# Baladi

The Journey
of an
Egyptian Street Dog

# Baladi

The Journey
of an
Egyptian Street Dog

## JOSH HINES

SNOW

WOLF

BOOKS

Published by Snow Wolf Books
Bowling Green, Kentucky

Manufactured print on demand

10 9 8 7 6 5 4 3 2 1

cover photo by Stephanie Hines-Fountain
back illustration by Blake Sims

# DEDICATION

Dedicated to Tena Cross and Anne Grubbs. My two biggest supporters in writing this book and you will both never be able to read it.

Thank you for your encouragement and believing in this story. I miss you both every day.

For the animals and people of ESMA. You are an inspiration to us all.

And for my Hogs. I hope you're proud of me.

# CONTENTS

# ACKNOWLEDGMENTS

To my wife Mandy. You brought the inspiration and motivation back into my life. I would have given up on this without you. Everything I do is for you and our little fur family.

To my kids. Sphyncus: the Athena to my Zeus. You were my destiny and I owe everything to you. You're the weirdest dog in the world and I wouldn't change a thing. The life opened up to me because of you was completely unimaginable. In an existence that has had billions of dogs, thank you for being alive at the same time as me. Chewie: the strongest boy in the entire world. Your fight is one of legend. Thank you for being my son, brother, and mentor. Boo: thank you for giving me back something I thought I had lost. You're the best friend and sister Sphyncus could have ever hoped to have. Mustachio: your timing was impeccable. Please stop peeing on things and just let me pet you. Gorgar: the weirdest cat I've ever known. Never stop Keekin'. Basil: the little Taffer. Keep jumping and chirping and making us laugh. Chewy cat: I miss your disgusting voice. Thank you for being the first cat to accept Sphyncus. Bengal: Thank you for filling a void and being a true sweetheart. The world is darker without you. Prissy: my first ever hog. You gave us 17 years of your sweet smile.

You always deserved better. E-Style: my soulmate. Thank you for teaching me everything worth knowing. You changed my entire view of animals and what love is. I will never stop dreaming of when we are together again.

To Mona and Bahra. You took a chance on me and I can never thank you enough. Without you this story wouldn't exist. You are my heroes and the heroes to thousands of animals. You have my endless respect and gratitude. I am forever your friend and forever in your debt.

To my ESMA family. Heidi: your love and dedication is a thing to behold. I am humbled by your compassion. Lia and Anne-Marie: your work behind the scenes is not unrecognized. ESMA can't function without you. To Kristen: this entire process started with you. Thank you for getting the ball rolling and having the confidence in me to hand over the reins to the website all those years later. To Susie and Julie: we've never met but we've been in contact for years. I know how important you are to the story of ESMA. To Mohamed, Walid, and all the other workers: you all do the dirty work every day. Thank you for always welcoming me back and treating me like one of your own. To Mohamed: thank you for all the rides. You're the best driver in Cairo.

To my little Cairo family. Kris: my mom away from home. Thank you for showing me the ropes and making me comfortable. Mohamed: my Egyptian brother. Always there for me. Heidi: my Egyptian sister with the beautiful voice. Over my trips to Cairo you've shown me a side that I never knew existed. Louby: a friend when I've needed one. Thank you for always listening and giving honest advice. Phaedra: for your encouragement. Having the support of an actress is the ultimate bragging right.

To my family and friends. Mom: you've been my biggest fan since the day I was born. I can always count on you to cheer me on. Smitty: I don't know that I would have found ESMA without you. Thank you for being the big brother I needed. My two Dads: I never know how to address you both without risk of offending. You both played a role in raising me to be the man I am and I'm eternally grateful. Stephanie: the best sister and photographer on the planet. You looking up to me gave me the confidence to succeed. David: you're not my cousin, you're my brother. And the best friend I'll ever have. Always will be. Garrett: you're also not a cousin but a brother. Thank you for taking the journey over with me and seeing ESMA for yourself. To Megan: throughout our travels you've been my friend, sister, and "wife." Seth: thank you for trusting me to take you to Egypt and experiencing ESMA .

To my editors and early readers. Stewie: you've been one of my best friends my entire life. Thank you for your brutal honesty. Carrie: you refined this book more than I ever could have. I wouldn't have seen it through without you. Jen: you came in at the finish line and give it the final touches. Shawna: thank you for reading an early draft that nobody had any business reading. This also gives me a chance to thank Ken for knowing me better than anyone else in the world.

To all the others that played a part. Iman Satori, Michael Farmer, Kevin Mercer, WBKO, VCRD, Randi Hunton, Tidball's, Chest Rockwell, Technology Vs Horse, and Bass Invaders.

Thanks to Jay Sizemore for the final print prep work.

To those I've lost along the way. Jeremy Pryor, Cory Smith, Tena Cross, and Anne Grubbs.

To everyone else that gave me support and was a part of this journey: I can't possibly list you all but I appreciate everything, no matter how small.

*Baladi*

## PREFACE

The scrawny, brown dog raced into Haram Street and almost immediately started to poop right in the middle of traffic. Surrounded by cars racing up then halting, horns blaring, and changing lanes with only an inch between them. Surely, one of them was about to plow into it.

Miraculously, the dog made it back to the sidewalk unscathed, as if it was surrounded by an invisible barrier. I can't explain it. I was sure the dog was going to be absolutely obliterated and all I could do was watch from five floors up.

Once back on the sidewalk things weren't any better. Children started chasing it while whipping some type of rope. The dog cried out and continued to flee as fast as a limping dog could. Adults were standing around doing nothing. Policemen just stood there. People walked by without a second glance. Everything was normal. There was a terrified dog being tormented and tortured and everyone behaved as if nothing out of the ordinary was going on.

I had seen enough.

Josh Hines

## Chapter 1

Brown. It's the only word that can describe flying into Cairo. Brown. The ground. The buildings. The horizon. Everything. I was traveling with my cousin David and our friend Megan, making our way across Europe into Egypt. Despite this being my twelfth country at the time, I was completely unprepared for the next three days of culture shock and emotional trauma that awaited me.

We started toward the airport exit and were immediately bombarded by salesmen and their tour packages. One particular gentlemen was unshakeable and accompanied us down the entire hall. He told us all about the wonderful things he had to offer by showing us photocopied black and white pictures in clear plastic sleeves held in a white plastic binder. The tools of a real professional. There was almost a nervousness about him, but that didn't dissuade him from making his pitch. He was a living caricature of a person you expected to find selling tours.

"My friends, I have tour for you. Take you to see the piddamids. To see the sfeenkus. This one to Saqqara. To Memphis."

"No, no, no we already have tours booked." It was a lie, we had arranged nothing but a hotel. The man's thick accent made it difficult to understand some of the things he said. The "piddamids" were obviously the pyramids but we had no idea what the "sfeenkus" was.

"My friends, I offer you a ride to your hotel, yes? Very cheap." The one way ride from the airport to the hotel was to cost us 140 LE. In 2010 that was about 25 USD.

"He will take you from here," the nervous salesman said, as a younger, more confident man approached. There was a look in his eyes like he was expecting something but I had never heard of tipping somebody for essentially calling another person over to perform the task, so we stiffed him.

Once outside, there was a sense of arrival to finally breathe in the hot air of that ancient land I had imagined all my life. Heat with low humidity. A vastly different type of heat from our home state of Kentucky where the humidity feels like you're always walking through a heavy, moist film in the summer.

The car we were escorted to was just a regular car, not any sort of sanctioned taxi with markings on it. A larger man got out and put our bags into the trunk. David and Megan filed into the back and I walked toward the passenger seat. The man that walked us through the airport approached me and said something that I still quote to this day.

"Now is time for giving me tips if you like."

Recalling the look I was given by the initial salesman, an alarm sounded in my head that this was only the beginning of what we were going to be dealing with our next few days. I ended up giving him a small tip because I didn't want to create some type of situation where we had our luggage in the trunk and had angered the driver or his partner.

The driver didn't speak much English, but motioned for us to roll our windows down and turned on the radio. The opening riff to AC/DC's 'You Shook Me

All Night Long' started up. I turned back to smirk at David and Megan at the absurdity of it. If you had asked me what the first song I thought I might hear in Egypt would be, never in a million years would I have guessed something as sexually suggestive as 'You Shook Me All Night Long.' That entire scene plays over in my head every time I've heard it since. "Now is time for listening to AC/DC if you like."

The ride to our hotel was quite an adventure. Cairo is the 15th largest city in the world and the entire thing is one big traffic jam with no discernible rules. Absolute chaos at every turn. Roundabouts feature cars going face to face with each other rather than all in the same direction. Cars are coming from all angles in a cacophony of horns blaring and people shouting, forcing their way between the cars driving perpendicular to them. Buses packed to the brim with people hanging their arms out the windows. Trucks with who knows what wrapped up tight and stacked, teetering eight feet high in the bed. Scooters with entire families squeezed onto them. Horses and donkeys calmly pulling carts while surrounded by total mayhem. The occasional camel being ridden by somebody on a cell phone. And, of course, the pedestrians attempting to cross through all of it. They may be the bravest people I have ever seen. Literally risking their lives just to get to the other side of the road like the most intense game of Frogger ever played.

The state of decay of some of the roads, the dirt lots filled with garbage and stray animals, the overwhelming brown-ness of the buildings and all the surroundings all left me a bit on edge.

After about an hour of experiencing full speed—stop—full speed—stop—full speed—stop for pedestrian —full speed, almost get hit—stop, it was getting into the evening hours and our driver started to get anxious. He motioned to the car next to us to roll their window down then pulled out a printout of our hotel reservations. He had no idea where our hotel was and now had to backtrack.

When we finally arrived at the hotel, rather than popping the trunk the driver stuck his hand out for a tip. This was the exact type of behavior I was worried about. If the guy that simply walked us to the taxi expected a tip, certainly the driver that didn't even know where he was going was also going to want one.

I had initially withdrawn only 200LE at the airport, which was around 35 US dollars. The fee for the taxi service and the tip for our escort didn't leave me with much remaining so I forked over what I had while David and Megan gave him a similar share. The driver looked at us sternly and said, "This is too small." His body language made it obvious he wasn't going to move until we paid him more. All our bags were stuck in the trunk, completely at his mercy. David handed him some more bills and the driver mumbled "Is okay" before getting out of the car to unload our bags. We checked into the HUSA Pyramids (now known as Gawharet Al-Ahram Hotel) and scoped out the pool before heading up to our room on the fifth floor.

Room 503 faced the front of the hotel, overlooking the sidewalk and street down below. There was a mosque directly next door, separated only by a small alley. From our room's window you could see the green light on the minaret. You could also hear every salah (prayer) call. All 5 of them. Every day. Loud and clear.

Our room was laid out like any normal hotel room except it had a third bed right next to the window. As fate would have it, that bed was to be mine and this story might not exist had it played out any other way.

By the time we settled in, it was getting late and we weren't feeling particularly adventurous our first night so we went to the top floor to eat at the hotel restaurant. Walking out onto the balcony, we were treated to our first view of the Pyramids of Giza. Seeing those original ancient wonders of the world looming over a modern city was surreal--the past and present engaged in an unending battle for the horizon.

Before coming to Cairo, we'd spent the previous two weeks in London, Rome, and Athens. Everything we saw in those places paled in comparison to what we were standing in the presence of that first night in Cairo. The Pyramids are nothing short of majestic.

David is two years younger than me and we've been best friends since the day he was born. Neither of our families had much money when we were growing up so family vacations were typically a trip to the beach in the summer or maybe camping. In high school, when my friends were signing up for school trips to Europe, it was never even a consideration for us. Thousands of dollars for a two-week vacation was just out of the question. Once we got to college, David and I decided to take out extra-large loans one semester and go to Europe for three weeks during Christmas break. The fabled "travel bug" bit us and we became addicted. After that we based our entire lives around saving up enough money to see new parts of the world every year.

The exchange David and I shared on the HUSA balcony looking at the Pyramids was similar to a moment we shared during our first trip overseas together. In late December 2004, we stood at the top of the Eiffel Tower at night, admiring the lights and atmosphere of Paris. We confided in each other our appreciation of all our years together and how we had somehow ended up there. Then in May 2010, standing on that balcony and looking at the Great Pyramids, we shared that feeling again. We had goals and found a way to achieve them. I can't speak for David, but I felt immense pride.

While marveling at the Pyramids we also got our first glimpse of something else interesting: every rooftop had an obscene amount of trash on it. Bags of trash, old furniture, random stray clothing, unidentifiable garbage, whatever you can imagine that would be thrown out. I was later told that it's common because garbage collection is an issue in Cairo and the roof gets it out of sight. Though once you're up high enough and actually see it, it's impossible to overlook. Nothing like pure waste to potentially soil every breathtaking view you may have.

Dinner that night was relatively tame. In my personal experience, when you're a vegetarian struggling to make sense of a menu in a foreign language, you tend to eat a lot of pasta because it's safe. There's almost always a pasta offered with no meat and you don't have to worry about local water being used to wash something that might make you sick. So pasta it was. Safe and ordinary for our first night. An omen of things to come.

Back in the room, we turned on the TV to find that the only channel coming in clearly was playing *Aladdin: The Return of Jafar.* I don't think there's anything in the world that could have stopped our laughter. It wasn't necessarily that it was on, it's that this straight to video sequel of a Disney cartoon filled with stereotypes about the region of the world we just so happened to be in was pretty much our only option. If we were to watch TV, we literally had to watch *Aladdin: The Return of Jafar.* Of course it was in Arabic so that made it even better, the full experience. Maybe two weeks of jet lag and new cultures every few days had us all a bit loopy, but *The Return Jafar* was the most hilarious thing in the world at the time. Maybe Egypt wasn't going to be so bad after all.

## Chapter 2

After a long night of being repeatedly awoken by car horns and prayer calls, morning finally came. Having arrived in the late afternoon the previous day and flying out at midnight the following night, this was to be our only full day in Egypt. According to the website we booked through, we were supposed to interpret this as 3 days in Cairo. Clearly not enough time and we would be reminded of that quite often.

We left the hotel around 7 a.m. to avoid the sun as best as we could. The temperature was set to be over 100 degrees Fahrenheit, but at least the humidity would be low. One hundred degrees in Egypt feels better than 80 degrees in Kentucky humidity. At home, I can walk outside and immediately sweat in the heavy southern air. In Cairo, I could feel the heat on my skin, but it was tolerable.

The main road that our driver had gotten turned around on the night before is Haram Street. HUSA Pyramids has a little crescent moon-shaped access road in front of it called Umm Al Abtal Square that connects to Haram, creating a half-circle slab of concrete between the two. Other than a few trees and a couple of benches, it's basically just a wide, dirty sidewalk. While walking across it that morning to catch a taxi, I spotted a scrawny, light brown dog stumbling around a truck parked by the curb. The poor thing looked fairly young and appeared to be injured. A small group of people were standing nearby so I hoped it was with them.

Taxis were lined up all along the curb and we approached the first one we came to. Like our dinner the night before, we kept it safe and easy. No haggling. Like 90% of men in Egypt, our driver was named Mohamed. He quoted us an all-day price of $40, which seemed too good to be true. He was quite happy with the arrangement. Split amongst the three of us, we were quite happy with the deal, too.

For whatever reason, I always got stuck in the front sitting next to the driver. It had happened everywhere we had been and now it had happened twice in Cairo. The taxi was another "taxi" as it had no meter running. This was just a car, much like what we had taken from the airport. I wasn't exactly thrilled about possibly going through the same bullshit again, but at least we didn't have any luggage in the trunk that could be held hostage. As I put my seatbelt on, I turned around to David and Megan.

"Did you see that pitiful dog over there?"

"Yeah, I was hoping you didn't," Megan replied. The tone of her voice and look on her face told me she knew I was going to be thinking about that dog all day.

"My friends, where are you going?" Mohamed asked. "The Pyramids."

"Ah yes. The piddamids," he said with a grin. Mohamed's thick accent made it more difficult to communicate than I had anticipated. He understood us fine, we just couldn't understand him that well. Trying to make small talk turned into him listing the places he could take us to see after the Pyramids.

"I will take you to Saqqara, to Memphis, to see the sfeenkus." There was that word again. Sfeenkus.

Considering we could see the Pyramids from the roof of the HUSA, it didn't take long to reach them. As we pulled up, the car was approached by armed guards dressed all in white carrying assault rifles. They looked like they should have been in a James Bond movie hanging around a snow-covered base in the mountains. One of them pounded his fist down on the hood of the car. It wasn't really in anger but he was wanting something from Mohamed, at least his attention. The car stopped and a few words were said in Arabic, then Mohamed sped away towards the ticket booth. We weren't sure what had just happened. Nobody wants men with machine guns pounding on the hood of their car. Assured that Mohamed would be waiting for us when we were finished, we got out of the car and made towards the entrance.

David gave me an odd look. "What's that on your shoulder?"

"Huh?" I said tugging at my shirt to get a look.

"I don't know, maybe dirt or something from the seatbelt?" he laughed.

"Well, shit. Yeah, I guess it is." The dark stripe ran down my shoulder and across part of my chest, exactly where the seatbelt would've been. No sense in getting worked up over a little seatbelt dirt. It hadn't been an official taxi we had gotten into and the price was so low I should have guessed it wasn't going to the cleanest ride—still it's funny looking back at pictures we took that morning and seeing that faint, blackish line go down my plain white t-shirt.

Wiping the seatbelt dirt down from a bold, black referee stripe to a more modest gray faded line, we bought our tickets to enter the Giza Plateau. I can't really describe walking up to The Pyramids for the first time. They're so big it's hard to take them in all at once. Good luck getting a close-up picture next to them while managing to fit one entire pyramid in.

The entire complex at Giza had a lot more to offer than I had previously thought. In addition to the Sphinx, which was much smaller than I expected, there were numerous smaller pyramids and tombs peppering the area. It's difficult to imagine what it all must have looked like in its original glory.

We came to Khufu's Pyramid (The Great Pyramid) first and, unfortunately, we couldn't go inside. After taking some pictures, we realized Khafre's Pyramid was open to the public so we started to make our way there. Almost immediately, we were approached by a small guy asking us if we wanted a camel ride. Classic Egyptian scam. We politely declined, but those guys hanging around the Pyramids are pros and don't take the first, second, or third 'no' for an answer. I'm not sure how many 'no's it would have taken—but we didn't have enough. The guy started showing us these little knockoff head wraps while his friends appeared out of nowhere to start putting them on our heads.

While still walking, albeit at a slower pace and repeating "no" over and over, I somehow found myself no longer walking but sitting on a camel. The very same camel I specifically did not want to ride. Megan was miraculously on the same camel seated behind me. I have no idea how it happened, it was all too quick. I couldn't even tell you who was on it first. It was as if we had teleported onto a kneeling camel that started to stand

up as soon as we realized what was happening. In the confusion, I saw that David was also on a camel seated in front of an Egyptian man. I'd never even ridden a horse before so I was pretty apprehensive about riding that camel. David at least had a buddy with him that knew what he was doing, Megan and I were on our own. The salesman was walking beside us, but I had the reigns and felt like I could fall off at any moment.
Seated on the camels there was certainly no reason to resist anymore, so we just went with it. We were already on the damned things and didn't know how to get off. Might as well enjoy the ride because it won't happen again and we would surely be paying for it. What followed was one classic Egyptian photo op after another as the guys on the ground led the camels around a series of pre-planned locations.

There's one photo of Megan and me sitting on the camel with one hand each in the air, cupped upside down over the peak of Khafre's Pyramid, exactly as the pharaoh must have imagined tourists would do all those years ago. Then it was David's turn. Then both camels next to each other while all three of us had our hands up together over a Pyramid. For their last trick, Megan sat on the camel alone while I stood on the ground holding the rope as if I'd been walking it and she was royalty. We were total rookies and they worked us over. I'm not going to say there isn't a piece of me that didn't somewhat enjoy it, but I would have never done it intentionally and I would never do it again. It was more, "let's make the best of an unfortunate situation rather than be a group of sourpusses."

Off in the distance we heard some shouting that had a ring of authority to it. Everyone looked over to see what appeared to be the white uniformed police riding towards us on horses, still shouting. Our camel guys quickly started speaking among themselves then all at once took to running. If we were uncomfortable sitting on slow walking camels, we were terrified bobbing around on them while they sprinted. I didn't think there was anything illegal about the camel guys being there and doing their thing but they clearly wanted nothing to do with the police. Much to my surprise, it didn't take long for the officers to give up their chase. I couldn't believe they would just stop their pursuit like that.

For the big camel finale, we were led somewhere a little out of the way to discuss payment. Since we were on two different camels, our group was strategically separated. I felt bad for David dealing with it alone. I knew he was going to get hustled.

"Are you happy? Make me happy." A catchy sales pitch from the instigator of the whole fiasco.

"I don't know what that means," I replied.

"My friend. Are you happy?"

"I guess."

"Make me happy."

This is where I learned a vital lesson when visiting somewhere with known scammers. Never keep all of your money in one place. As soon as I opened my wallet to dig out some Egyptian Pounds I could see the man's face light up. It was like a cartoon character when a light bulb flashes above his head. He saw we had cash money and we couldn't be cheapskates. His eyes were literally glowing and his smile was ear to ear. The best part was they didn't just want money, they started asking for anything we had.

"My friend, I can have this?" He pointed toward the lip balm I was applying.

"What? My chapstick? Why? No. Sorry." I was getting irritated at what felt like begging.

One of them motioned towards Megan and pointed at her sunscreen she had pulled out of her bag while digging for money. "What about this?"

"No. I need that more than you do," Megan scoffed.

"Where you from?" the man asked.

"Canada," I said with a smirk. It was the first time I had ever lied about being an American.

"My friend, I like your beard. You look Egyptian."

"Really? Then why don't any of you have one?" I asked him.

"I will teach you Arabic phrase. You say 'no, thank you.' 'La shukran.'" He was almost laughing because he knew we could've used that phrase about 15 minutes ago.

"La showcram." I repeated.

"No, no. La. Shukran."

"La shukran." Nailed it.

"Yes, yes, very good! You say this and people leave you alone. Welcome to Egypt!"

"Good to know. Thanks." I appreciated his game but I hated that we fell for it. We started walking to Khafre's Pyramid to finally go inside after this little side quest we had accidentally accepted, but the guy rushed up and interrupted again.

"My friend, what is this on your shirt?" he asked me.

"Dirt from the seatbelt in the taxi. I don't care." I was getting frustrated at his persistence. We weren't getting fooled a second time.

"He is bad driver. You shouldn't ride with him."

I didn't respond and kept walking.

"My friend, do you like this shirt? I will give it to you." He tugged at his own shirt as he kept walking alongside us.

"What? No. La shukran."

"Ha ha! Very good!" And just like that they were gone, making their way to pull a fast one on the next group of unsuspecting tourists.

One of the more understated visuals of the Giza Plateau is the city of Cairo sprawling from the desert. It's 'past meets present' separated by a small wall. The buildings of Cairo spread out in every direction as far as you can see in front of you. Nothing but sand and stone behind--like someone had drawn a line in the sand and said "time stops here." It made me wonder if in a few hundred years the city will finally cross that line and absorb the Pyramids into itself. Could high rises stand directly next to the Pyramids? I doubt it would ever come to something like that, but visiting places like Rome where cars drive within feet of the Colosseum makes you think about it. Modern Cairo is knocking on Khufu's door right now with the Pyramids Sound and Light Show and a paved roadway leading from the gate. How long until that roadway becomes multiple roadways, requiring gas stations and restaurants?

Feeling like we had seen what we came all the way to Egypt for, we headed back to the gate and found Mohamed waiting exactly where he had dropped us off. We told him we wanted to go back to the hotel for a few hours to rest and plan our next move. Maybe it was the jet lag from the last two weeks, maybe it was the heat—or maybe it was both—but we suddenly required time to recharge after the Pyramids. He was all too happy to agree to this. We had already paid for his services for the full day so this gave him the chance to go earn extra money on top of it.

We each retreated to our respective beds in the room and decided the Egyptian Museum would be next. In all honesty, I don't think any of us had really thought much past the Pyramids. The bulk of our odyssey was spent in Europe and we had closer to three full days in each of the other places we had been. Here, we had to cram everything in but we pulled it off fairly well. Cairo was almost more like a long layover on the way home rather than a full stop with time to explore. We came to see the Pyramids and quickly checked it off the list. Anything else would be a bonus.

Having made our plans, we each sat around snacking and reading, flipping through the channels on the TV hoping something else hilarious would come on. One by one, we each started to doze off.

I've always been a terrible sleeper—and I had the bed right by the window. If I slept at all, it wasn't much and it was very interrupted. Street noise, car horns, prayer call, a dog crying out.

"What the…" I sat up in bed and looked out the window. Did I just hear that? A dog crying out? In that traffic, my god, I hoped not.

There seemed to be a little bit of commotion happening on the sidewalk between the access road and Haram Street, the place I saw the little pitiful dog that morning. Two kids came running around a bench. One of them was swinging something that looked like a piece of rope or a small chain. It was hard to make out from the fifth floor.

"What are you doing?" I whispered to myself, as not to wake anyone. I feared I knew exactly what they were doing but I hadn't actually seen it yet.

The kids kept running. The one in the lead was whipping his rope relentlessly. Eventually they went behind a parked car where I couldn't see them anymore. A dog yelped out even louder and started running towards the street. It had a hobbled run. Something was clearly wrong with one of its legs. It was the same dog I had seen that morning.

"Goddamn it." It was heading straight into Haram Street. My heart sank into my stomach. The dog was about to run the gauntlet.

## Chapter 3

My mind was blank. I don't remember anything between walking out of our room and being on the street. It was like when you start daydreaming while driving then you suddenly come to and realize you have no memory of how you got there.

Every second I was away from the window was a moment too long. I had no idea what was happening on the street anymore. The dog could be dead by the time I got there. It could have run back into Haram Street and become a smear on the pavement. The kids could have chased it completely away. The kids could be beating it when I arrived. What would I do? Who would argue with the American tourist? Would there be consequences? Would I get into some sort of trouble? I'm positive those things must have gone through my head on some subconscious level, but none of them would deter me.

I felt the searing heat of the Cairo afternoon on my skin and my mind began racing as everything came back into focus. Crossing the little access road, I didn't see the dog anywhere. I don't remember even seeing the kids that were chasing it. If they weren't still abusing the dog then they were completely insignificant to me. Their entire lives were meaningless. Their parents were garbage for letting them behave that way and not teaching them any better. The dog was the only thing that mattered.

I looked all around the sidewalk. No luck. I looked into the street to make sure it wasn't flattened out there. Nope. I looked across the street to the other side to see if somehow it had made it over, onto the next level of Frogger. Not there either. I looked up and down the sidewalk. It was nowhere to be seen. Where was it? I can only imagine how my face looked. Distraught, angry, on the verge of tears. The dumb tourist.

I saw something move under a car parked against the sidewalk. I knelt to get a look and the concrete scorched my hands. It was the dog in an absolute panic, panting and whimpering with its eyes wide and tongue flopping about. Completely horrified. It was sort of sitting on its side leaning up with its head almost touching the bottom of the car. I had to get it out from under there, but how?

Approaching the car still crouched down, I realized how easily it could all go wrong. A dog that scared was likely to bite. If it didn't bite it was certainly not going to come out on the same side as me, which would then leave it to escape into the Haram Street traffic. It was suddenly a struggle to think clearly and come up with a plan. What was I even doing?

I creeped over to the side of the car and tried to sweet talk the petrified animal. I reached out slowly toward it. What an idiot I must have looked like. It had to be the most naïve, ineffective way of attempting to overcome the predicament we were in.Feet suddenly appeared on the other side of the car. Then they disappeared, followed by a door slam. The engine started. Did he not see me when he was walking up to it? What did he think I was doing? Did he not see the dog?

I stretched upward, looking into his window and yelled loud enough where he could hear me over all of the street noise. "Hey, there's a dog under your car! Hey! There's a dog under here! Let me get it out!"

I could tell by the look on his face he was surprised to see me and didn't understand anything I had said. I pointed down under his car. He turned it off, opened his door, and leaned out. The man looked under at the dog that was getting more hysterical by the second. The door shut and he leaned across the passenger seat toward me.

"I will drive over him without drive over him." It came out so completely serious while sounding like the most asinine thing a person could possibly say. It was at that exact moment the severity of the situation hit me. These people didn't care. Nobody cared. The dog meant absolutely nothing to them. It wasn't protected. Its life wasn't precious. It was just another obstacle and time was of the essence. They had people to scam and I was costing them a chance at some other tourist's Chapstick the longer I stood there with my jaw dropped open.

"I will drive over him without drive over him?" What in the world did that even mean? Apparently I was supposed to believe he would be able to move the car while the dog freaking out underneath just stayed put so the tires didn't go over it. That was without a doubt the stupidest thing I'd ever heard an adult human being say.

As I crouched there, staring blankly, the engine started back up and the guy put it in drive. The dog cried out in fear and shifted its weight trying unsuccessfully to get up. Instinctively I just started banging my fist on the passenger door. I didn't even realize what I was doing until I had already done it. The car went back into park and the driver started to get out. I stood up, readying myself for whatever confrontation I had just initiated. In my periphery a figure in all white started to appear. It was a police officer. There was a post of some kind further down the sidewalk where the access drive connected back to Haram Street. Even if the officer sided with the driver, at least I should get out of the situation without anything getting physical. Hopefully, anyway.

The driver was visibly irritated as he came around the back of the car. He started to say something but the officer cut him off. Score one for me, the officer sided with the tourist. I'm not sure every American officer would have done the same if it were an Arabic man banging on the side of a white man's car, but Egypt doesn't need a bad reputation when it comes to handling tourists. The two men exchanged words for a minute, then the driver stepped back toward the trunk while the officer motioned for me to lean down with him.

He started making sounds and reaching for the dog from the front of the car while I did it from the passenger side. The dog must have felt even more threatened by being surrounded because it was getting a little snappy and crying out. Eventually it maneuvered out from under the car on the driver's side, exactly where I didn't want it to go. The driver was just a spectator at that point, probably humored by the fact that the dog I was desperately trying to save just ran into Haram Street.

I stood up and the dog whizzed past us, hobbling at breakneck speed. The officer had played his role and was done. He motioned for the driver to move along and turned to walk away, heading towards the post he came from. I instantly made for the dog.

It had run across the sidewalk, across the little access drive, and under another goddamn car that was parked next to the alley running down the side of the hotel. Crouching down again, I could see the dog wasn't even slightly calmed down. Sure, I knew it was away from the intense traffic and could rationalize that it was safer, but a dog doesn't think like that. It felt in just as much danger as ever, as well as being relentlessly pursued by some strange man.

Trying to get the dog out from under that second car was hopeless. I began to put together how futile the whole thing was. I didn't have the faintest idea what I would do if the dog did crawl out from under there and came up to me. I couldn't take it up to the room. I didn't have any food or water with me. I guess I just wanted to comfort it. I don't know. You don't think about those things in the heat of the moment, but after a few minutes of scrambling around I was developing a little more mental clarity.

A little boy came over and looked at me, smiling. He had a stick in his hands. At maybe 5-years-old, he was too small to be one of the kids I saw chasing the dog so I smiled back at him. He said something in Arabic to me and I just shrugged.

"I'm trying to get this dog. Dog? Dog?" I said pointing under the car.

The boy got low to the car and made this "psh psh psh" sound at the dog. He was clearly amused by me. Judging by the kids chasing the dog, the people around doing nothing, the man wanting to drive over it, I suppose I had to be pretty amusing to everyone that saw anything that had transpired in the past five to ten minutes.

"Look at the dumb foreigner. What a fool he is for giving a shit! We don't have time for that! Now is time for giving me tips if you like!"

Making no progress on getting the dog out from under the car, the boy decided to throw his stick under there. Of course, he hit it. The dog howled out and instantly squirmed to get out from under the car.

As I stood up I heard laughter from down the alley. There was an older man carrying what looked like rolls of carpet.

"Welcome to Egypt!" he yelled to me.

That was the second time I had heard that phrase in the last few hours and it certainly wouldn't be the last time I would hear it. It was belittling, each time more so than the last. I came all the way to Egypt to be mocked because I don't think animal abuse is acceptable. Amazing.

I turned just in time to see the dog run into the mosque next door. A smile, maybe more of a smirk, came across my face. The dog had sought refuge in the mosque. I wondered how long it would last. I briefly contemplated going in after it. My smirk disappeared as I thought more about it. If those kids were just casually beating a dog, an adult was going to just casually "drive over him without drive over him," carpet-man was going to just welcome me to Egypt for my troubles, how would somebody in the mosque react? The last thing I wanted to do was get involved with a person whose religion I didn't understand that maybe just had their prayers interrupted.

Before I made any sort of decision I would possibly regret, the dog came running like mad out of the mosque with a voice shouting behind. It took off away from me as fast as it could on that little bum leg. A brief jog after it was all I had in me. Even injured, the dog was too fast for me and already too far away. I lost it.

Standing there staring aimlessly at where the dog used to be I finally started to put everything together in my head. Rage. Sadness. Despair. Hopelessness. What seemed like an infinite number of feelings all fighting for space right up front. I had no past experiences to compare to.

I slowly made my way back into the hotel, not making eye contact with anyone at the desk. I was curious if they saw any of what happened and, if I had looked their way, would they have hit me with another "welcome to Egypt." I shuddered to think about it.

Chapter 4

When I got back in the room, David and Megan were sitting on their respective beds wide awake. I can only imagine how confused they were. I told them everything as it had happened. It was obvious it would affect me for what little time remained of our vacation.

A little while later we went down to meet our driver, Mohamed. I looked around the sidewalk for the dog, pointing out to David and Megan the different locations in which things had happened. The dog was long gone and I had to try to move on as well.

HUSA wasn't close to any other major sites in Cairo besides the Pyramids, so we had a little bit of a drive to get downtown to The Egyptian Museum. A drive spent mostly in silence, staring out at what had quickly become the least favorite place I'd ever visited. Things that hadn't really bothered me 24 hours ago now felt like travesties.

Traffic, garbage everywhere, rundown buildings, donkeys pulling carts, the brownness—everything was getting under my skin. It took close to 30 minutes to reach our destination. The only things that made me look up again with any appreciation at all were seeing Cairo Tower as we crossed the Nile and going past Tahrir Square, home of the major political demonstrations and protests of Egypt.

The old Egyptian Museum looks like a government building, but is a pale reddish color, very striking and out of place amongst all the brown. There are two Sphinx-like statues outside, each one flanking a small pool with shrubbery in the middle.

As unique as the building looked, it was quickly time for more disappointment. When we bought our tickets, they took our cameras from us. That has changed over the years, but back then no cameras were allowed inside. We were all uncomfortable with it and confused as to why it was necessary. Our entire trip was on our cameras and it made us nervous. We had encountered too many untrustworthy people and I had no faith in any Egyptian outside of our driver.

Our last stop before Cairo had been Athens, where we visited the National Archeological Museum. Inside that museum I saw things that blew my mind. I'm a huge Greek mythology fan; the Iliad is my favorite book. Seeing the Mask of Agamemnon and taking my picture next to it was a dream come true. The Antikythera Mechanism is housed in that museum--an ancient Greek analogue computer dating back to around 87 BC. It was incredible to see and photograph. Arrowheads from the Battle of Thermopylae, best known to people from the comic and movie 300. I could list things off all day. We saw those things and, better yet, got to take pictures of them to remember the experience. Not happening in Cairo.We were shocked at how everything was displayed. Countless items were labeled with handwritten plain white notecards, most of which, in the English portions, were very hard to read. I was hoping for a distraction to take my mind off the dog, but I didn't even know what I was looking at most of the time. My negativity had bled into David and Megan and the majority of our museum experience was spent making snarky comments about everything. We were all completely over the museum, the city, and the country. Just killing time until we could go home.

Towards the back was the King Tut exhibit. In a little room to itself, it was by far the nicest and most well-kept display. Everything in there is so clean and shiny that it almost looks fake. Even while acting like an ass about everything else, I had to appreciate the Tut room. Tutankhamun's mask is one of the most beautiful physical objects I have ever laid eyes on. It's in immaculate condition, the very definition of pristine. That one item makes the entire museum worth visiting. I wish I had a picture of it more than I could ever say. Even now that cameras are allowed in the museum you still can't take pictures of that exhibit. In that instance, and that instance only, the battered Mask of Agamemnon beats out the flawless mask of King Tut every day of the week.

While waiting for Mohamed to pick us up, I put some thought into everything that had happened that day. The Pyramids of Giza and the Sphinx would be the only things in Egypt I appreciated seeing in the moment. The only things that didn't have the distraction of animal abuse tainting my mood as I looked at them. We came halfway around the world, spent two weeks visiting some of the most amazing places on the planet, and it all felt irrelevant. Some of the most important places in history, places I had only dreamed I would go, and all of it meant nothing. My dream vacation with my two best friends was ruined. Egypt had broken me down in a mere 24 hours. I had never felt that way in my life.

Mohamed finally rolled up in his dirty-seatbelt-mobile. "Where are we going next, my friends? Yes?"

"I think we're going back to the room. We're pretty tired."

"I can take you to Saqqara, to Memphis. Yes?"

"No, just back to the hotel."

"Where are you going tomorrow? Yes?"

"Tomorrow we go home."

"What?"

"Yeah, we go home tomorrow night."

"How long you in Egypt?"

"Three days," I said, letting out a deep breath, hoping Mohamed would get the hint.

"Three days?! Is too short, is too short." He was almost scolding us.

"Yeah, we leave tomorrow night, late. We have some time in the morning but I don't know what we're going to do."

"My friends, still too much to see. I will come by and pick you up tomorrow. Take you to Saqqara, to Memphis. Yes?"

"I don't know what we're doing tomorrow. Probably hanging around the hotel and resting." I didn't know it at the time but I was making decisions for the group as to what we would be doing. Nothing. Just waiting to leave.

"You have to come back. Is not enough time."

"Yeah, maybe one day," I lied to him. I had no intention of ever going back. As an animal lover, vegetarian, dog owner--this was clearly not the place for me.

Trying to make small talk back and get off the subject of our time in Egypt, I decided to ask Mohamed a question. He would give the most bizarre answer I'd ever heard. So much in fact that I still don't know that I understood what he said or meant.

"So do you ever travel? Like outside of Cairo or Egypt?"

"Eh, sometimes I like to park over there and"— insert unintelligible words here. He was pointing to a parking lot we were passing by. After looking at the lot, I turned to look back at David and Megan. Nobody understood.

"Wait," I cut him off mid-sentence. "I mean, do you travel in your time away from work? Like, do you ever get to go outside of Cairo or even Egypt anywhere? Where do you like to go?"

"I like to go park there sometimes and sit when I wait for picking people up." He had the same look on his face as when he was offering to take us to Saqqara and Memphis. Sort of a mix between matter of fact and attempting to convince. Totally serious.

That's about the last thing I specifically remember talking with Mohamed about. I was utterly confused by his answer and I didn't know what else to say. Did he not understand my question, even when I asked a second time? Did he really get no time off work —so he has a particular parking lot he enjoys sitting in? I could only assume that was the case. Considering the poverty we had seen in Cairo, I guess it made sense that he worked all the time and it was his entire life. He connected with this parking lot and the view it provided while waiting to pick up tourists like us. I wondered if he had been in this parking lot both times he had waited for us that day.

My problems seemed insignificant by comparison. My normal day-to-day life problems, not this dog situation. I was still very upset about that and nothing anyone could say about their station in life in Egypt could justify what I had seen. Having said that, I felt incredibly sorry for Mohamed.

He spent the rest of the drive randomly pointing out things we were passing. Maybe he was hoping we would want to see them and he could pick us up again later or the next day. I had a hard time making out a lot of what he was saying so I usually just agreed or nodded. If he smiled when he said it then I smiled when I nodded back. Sometimes he would tell us some history or how to pronounce something in Arabic. Occasionally he would say something about the Pyramids or Sfeenkus or Saqqara. Listening to him go on and on distracted me from the horrible traffic and how impossible it was to find any rhyme or reason to the flow of it.

We arrived at HUSA Pyramids and said our goodbyes to Mohamed the driver and his dirty seatbelts. He seemed a little sad to see us go and, looking back on it, I'm a little sad we didn't spend more time utilizing his services. We had paid him for a full day so he came out ahead as there was plenty of time left in the day to take on new riders. He was a good guy, I hope he eventually got to see more than just that parking lot.

When we got out of the car I glanced to the right, down the access road, and saw a dog laying underneath the back of a car. It was either asleep or dead and there were bits of food scattered under the car around it. I didn't get close enough to see for sure if it was even breathing, much less if it was the same dog. I can't explain why but I just didn't have it in me to approach it. After all the chasing that took place in the morning, if it was the same dog I just didn't want to disturb it. It was finally at peace.

It took me a long time to admit it to anyone, but the truth was at that moment I secretly hoped the dog was dead. If what I had witnessed earlier was that dog's normal day-to-day life then I thought it might be best if perhaps somebody poisoned the food and put it out of its misery. Better to get a good meal, go to sleep with a full belly, and just never wake up. What did it have to wake up to? Being beaten? Chased? Playing Frogger across Haram Street until it finally lost?

I was ashamed of myself for wishing that on any living thing, especially the dog that I was so invested in, but I couldn't help it. I had spent the entire day distracted and obsessing over it instead of appreciating the historical wonders inches from my face—but when it was finally laying right there in front of me I just wanted it to be dead. I had no idea at all of what to do for it. Earlier in the day there was the rush of trying to save it from the kids, the street, and the cars. The tension of the moment didn't let me formulate full thoughts on what would come next. I just wanted to save it from the present situation. Now that the present situation was simply sleeping under a car surrounded by food I recognized that there was no 'what's next.' I had been living in my own head all day but that same mind space was completely devoid of any sort of real plan. So, I shamefully wished it was just dead and both of our problems were over. The pain and suffering of living as a dog in Egypt was over for the little, scrawny, hobbled creature, and the overwhelming burden I had of not knowing how to realistically help it could be lifted from my shoulders.

I don't know if David or Megan saw it laying there. I didn't point it out. We went up to the room and I have no memory of anything else that happened the rest of the day.

## Chapter 5

I don't know what happened to me overnight but I woke up with a different attitude about everything. I wouldn't say I no longer felt defeated, but I most definitely didn't want to spend the entire day moping.

While at breakfast, I did what previously seemed impossible and concocted a plan. I would cut down a plastic bottle into a water bowl, take some meat from the buffet, and attempt to feed the dog.
David and Megan got a good chuckle watching the militant vegetarian smuggle meat slices into his shoulder bag. They weren't laughing at my plan or my motives--they were laughing at my determination to do something incredibly stupid by further investing myself in a random street dog.

The day seemed to drag on forever. Despite my better attitude and optimism regarding the dog, we still had a negative energy around us so we ultimately spent our last day just killing time until our flight. Nobody wanted anything to do with Cairo anymore but we were stuck there until 9 P.M., when we would catch a taxi to the airport.

We walked around the immediate area outside the hotel to find there was nothing worth seeing. There was the mosque we didn't want to go in and the guy with the carpets down the alley; I can't tell you anything else that was around. There was no desire to get another taxi to ride around in the pandemonium and get scammed wherever we ended up. Nobody saw the dog anywhere so we just went back inside.

The HUSA lobby had some little souvenir shops so I bought little trinkets for people back home. Rather than getting something more authentic we took the easy, safe route again by buying from our hotel lobby. How embarrassing to look back at.

There was the small pool on the other side of the lobby but we declined to get in it. Despite bringing bathing suits exclusively for that pool, suits that took up prime real estate in our luggage since we each only took one carry-on bag, we just didn't want to swim anymore. That might be fun and we weren't having any of that.

We made no attempts at finding bona fide Egyptian food in an authentic restaurant somewhere. Instead, we were generic and ate at the hotel again. We followed up all that excitement by sitting around the room reading, watching TV, snacking, and napping. Periodically somebody would check the window and look for the dog. Despite our handling of everything else, I wasn't about to give up on that.

We did see one humorous thing. Some kids had made their way to the grass median in the middle of Haram Street and were playing soccer. It was maybe six feet wide at most but they were trying to play in it. One fall in either direction at the wrong time could mean certain, immediate death. I didn't care. They were likely the same kids I had seen chasing and hitting the dog. I didn't want them to die and I definitely didn't want to see it happen with my own eyes, but I also just didn't care about them. And apparently neither did their parents.

Eventually their ball went into the road and got annihilated by a passing car. It was the funniest thing I had seen in two weeks. Payback, you little bastards. One thing I learned from watching those kids chase the dog is that they were relentless. So instead of calling it a day after the soccer ball, they took up wrestling. Right there in the middle of Haram Street, surrounded by death machines whizzing by. They were slamming each other into the grass and rolling around, almost acting like normal kids. I might have laughed with them rather than at them, but I was feeling too burned by any and all children I had encountered in the area. Maybe one of them would get hurt and I'd get to see them cry like they had made the dog cry. I was ashamed of myself for thinking it.

It's somewhat humiliating to think we spent our last day in Egypt behaving the way we did and I have to admit that I've always felt responsible for it. The situation with the dog the day before didn't just ruin my trip, I let it ruin David and Megan's as well. I wish we could go back in time and spend that last day differently. Flag down another Mohamed and get another seatbelt dirt stain on my shirt. Sweating it out in a car without air conditioning and navigating the most insane traffic in one of the world's most massive cities. He could finally take us to see Saqqara and Memphis. Maybe the Khan El Khalili bazaar or the Citadel. We could go up inside Cairo Tower and have dinner in the rotating restaurant. Squeezing in as much as possible then just sleep on the flight home. It's what we did everywhere else we had been.

In the end, we did none of those things. We decided that we had done what we came to do and that would be good enough. We briefly experienced a culture we were too proud to admit we were intimidated by and we saw the Pyramids of Giza. The three of us had stood in the presence of one of the Seven Wonders of the World and we should be satisfied by that. We even got to see the Egyptian Museum, King Tut's death mask, and Cairo Tower. Bonuses! I tried to convince myself that there was nothing at all to feel regretful about. It had been nearly two weeks since we left the US. Not the longest I've ever traveled overseas, but this one had been jam packed. We were physically and mentally exhausted. I was personally on the verge of emotional exhaustion. We just cashed in before it got worse.

Sometime around 7 P.M., mere hours before boarding our plane home never to return to this hellhole of animal cruelty, David was taking video of the traffic out of the hotel window and spotted the dog being kicked away by some people on the sidewalk. I quickly put the bowl, a water bottle, and meat into my shoulder bag. It was now or never.

## Chapter 6


My heart was racing as I exited the hotel. Over 24 hours of agony and obsession was hopefully about to pay off. I made my way down the sidewalk, past some people sitting on benches. The sky was getting darker and the heat was subsiding a bit. Calm conditions.

When I got within 20 feet of the dog, I slowed down and tried to pretend I was just minding my business, hoping I wouldn't scare it off. I walked a bit closer and sat down on the sidewalk. Trying to remain relaxed so the dog wouldn't pick up on my true intentions, I began to just look at it for a few seconds. It got up and started to stagger away but only went a few feet before sitting down again. No matter how interested in me it may have been, fear had taught it better. This dog had no reason to trust anyone so I had to be careful. I was curious if it recognized me from the day before.

I sat my bag down and pulled out the bowl. The dog's curiosity was growing, as it began to stare back at me. I poured some water and slid the bowl on the dirt toward the dog. It wagged its tail nervously. It wanted the water but I was too close. The dog grabbed the bowl in its mouth and tried to carry it off. Water slung all over the ground leaving nothing to drink. It stepped away from me again.

Next, I pulled some meat out and tossed a piece over. That got its attention. Snatching up the first piece out of the dirt, the dog looked at me again. I tossed another piece over, this one a little closer to me than the first. That would be my strategy—lure the dog closer and closer by tossing the meat shorter distances each time. A classic with a proven track record. Little by little the dog got nearer to me. When the meat was gone I grabbed up the water bowl and the dog lumbered forward a little bit more, stepping up on the edge of the sidewalk I was sitting on. I poured a second round of water and sat the bowl next to me.

The dog stepped down off the sidewalk into the dirt again and turned a circle, stumbling and sniffing at the ground most of the way. I picked up the bowl and slid it across the dirt once more, this time scooting myself away right after to give it some space. The dog came forward and started drinking, only stopping to look up at the sound of a car horn that was particularly close. Looking at the road then back at me, the dog's tail went in a full helicopter spin as it licked its lips.

It stumbled a little further away next to the water spill. Even while its tail was still happily going, the dog had its head hunched down like it was afraid I could strike it at any moment. Determined to pet it, I leaned forward and stuck out my closed fist at full arm's length, holding it there, hoping it would come toward me. It took a few steps closer, gingerly walking on that front leg.

Right around then I saw how badly it was hurt. The right front leg had a small bulge in the forearm and there was never any weight put on it. If it had to touch the ground it would do so very quickly, like a person who was trying to walk after just rolling an ankle. It looked as if it had a hard time balancing, always swaying a little bit and stepping side to side while moving forward. Its right ear was laid down on the side of its head, stiff and motionless, while the left ear stood up and bobbed about like a normal dog ear. The bad ear and bad leg were on the same side of the body, perhaps it had absorbed serious trauma on that side. I started to wonder what was wrong with it that I couldn't see.

The dog looked at me as if conflicted, wanting to come check me out but not trusting me yet. That's fair, it had no reason to trust anyone. Tail still going strong, the dog looked around—at me, then the ground, then the street—sniffing at the ground as if playing shy. I continued to hold out my closed hand and the dog would periodically stare at it, like it knew not to take its eyes off a fist. That front right leg was just flailing about, dangling centimeters above the ground while it decided what to do. Stepping closer, then back again. Eventually it sat down right on the spilled water but even the act of sitting looked to be a struggle. Something had to be wrong with a back leg or its hips to cause it to sit in such a way.

With its body stretched out a little more I could clearly see its ribs. There were numerous small spots on the legs completely devoid of hair that looked like they could've been cigarette burns. It wasn't as brown as I had originally thought, more of a light sandy color, but it was difficult to tell under all the filth. There was a little pinkish spot on its nose, almost shaped like a distorted heart. I couldn't tell how young it was but it was nowhere near an adult. Older than a puppy for sure, but unquestionably under a year.

It was sitting there biting at itself, but everything seemed like such a chore. It couldn't quite turn around normally to bite at its back, like everything was just very stiff. It started swinging that front right leg around by its head like it wanted to scratch that hard, flattened ear but the leg just couldn't do it. The leg swung at me a couple of times while the dog stared, almost like it was playing. Then back to biting at itself.

A young woman approached from across the street. It was written all over her face that she was intrigued by what was going on over on this side of Haram with me and the dog so she took the chance and beat Frogger level 1 to come find out for herself. She was dressed in typical attire from head to toe aside from having long sleeves under her shirt and a hijab. I confess I was equally intrigued by her and what she might say. I was about to have my first in depth conversation with an Egyptian that most likely didn't want money from me.

"Hallo, where are you from?" she asked in a thick but endearing accent with a gigantic smile.

"The U.S. Kentucky."

"Oh, like Kentucky Fried Chicken," she responded with a laugh.

"Uh, yeah. That's what everyone says." I hate it when people in a foreign country bring up KFC as their first association with Kentucky and it happens literally everywhere in the world.

She then asked, "What are you doing?"

"What do you mean? With the dog?"

"Yes, why are you doing this?"

"Well, uh, I love dogs," I answered. "I hate seeing one like this, starving and in bad shape. It's pitiful. Why does no one care?"

"Is normal here," she said with a shrug.

"This is not normal where I'm from."

"No?" she asked.

"No. We have strays but people usually try to help them. Maybe take them to a shelter or something. Yesterday I saw kids chasing this dog and hitting it. Their parents were just sitting there watching. I've never seen anything like that before. A guy tried to drive his car over it."

She gave me this innocent but almost embarrassed smile and said my three least favorite words: "welcome to Egypt," combined with a little shrug.

I had to bite my tongue. Saying, "welcome to Egypt," does not excuse any of the behavior I had witnessed towards the dog or the scam artists working around Giza, but everyone here seemed to accept it like it was a 'get out of jail free' card on Monopoly.

"Yeah, I keep hearing that, 'welcome to Egypt,'" I rolled my eyes. "So, why does nobody care about animals like this?"

"Look at it, it's dying." The look on her face showed no sympathy for the dog.

"I don't think it's dying, it's not that bad off. It's hurt, though. And hungry. I wish I could help it." It's like I was trying to convince her that I was right and she was wrong. "Is it like this everywhere over here? Not just Cairo, but all of Egypt?"

"Yes, people here don't have money or time to take care of animals."

"But that's no reason to be cruel. Just leave them alone then."

"Is baladi dog. Nobody wants them."

"A what? Ballady dog?" I had never heard of this breed before.

"Yes. Baladi. It means like, local dog. Street dog."

"Ah, ok. We just call them strays or mutts in America."

"Yes, is same thing. They come from the desert. People don't like them. They are aggressive."

"This dog is not aggressive. Look at it. It's the people I've seen that are aggressive."

She giggled a little, more so out of embarrassment than finding it funny. There was a massive societal divide between us. We came from two different worlds, seeing eye to eye just wasn't going to happen.

The young woman pointed out two officers at the post down the sidewalk to the right and how they were watching us, laughing. We slowly made our way over while still chatting. The dog followed us, keeping a little distance but making sure we didn't get too far away.

One of the officers was middle aged and the other was a bit younger, probably in his early twenties. The older one had no interest in us once we got there, but the younger man was still smiling and laughing a little. Neither officer spoke any English so I asked my new friend to translate.

"What's he laughing at?"

"He thinks it's funny. He's not laughing at you but he says he has never seen anything like this before."

Okay, I guess that's fine. He didn't look like an asshole so I just took the woman at her word. Honestly, he looked friendly, friendlier than the officer that helped me yesterday had been.

"Could you ask him how long that dog has been around here?"

They spoke in Arabic for a few seconds then she turned back to me. "He says it has been here a while. It's here every day."

"Every day." I repeated. "Is anyone ever with it?"

Turning to the officer then back to me. "No, is alone. It lives on the street."

"Okay, could you ask him one more thing for me?"

"Of course." She seemed genuinely happy to help and the officer didn't seem to mind either. The first two honestly helpful people I had met and they weren't expecting tips.

"Ask him if he knows what's wrong with it. It has that bad leg and that ear that doesn't go up. Something happened to it."

A minute later: "He says he doesn't know. People chase it away, sometimes hit it."

I shook my head in disgust. They both looked embarrassed. "Thank you. And tell him 'thank you,' too. Maybe he can keep an eye out on this dog for me from now on." I said it with a smile and the woman spoke again to the officer. He smiled back in what looked like amusement. I knew he wouldn't do it but maybe he would at least stop people from hitting it. We said our goodbyes and I turned my attention back to the dog.

It laid down in the dirt and rolled over on its back in total submission. This was it, the show of trust I had been working and waiting for.

45

Finally, I could see the dog was no longer an "it" but a female. I knelt down and rubbed her belly very lightly. She had a body like a greyhound—a skinny waist and deep chest. Her hair was smooth and soft. Having no idea what other injuries she might have I had to be cautious. The thought of something bad happening after all I had gone through to get close to her was a nightmare. The last thing I wanted to do was touch a rib that could be broken or rub a spot that might be sore. If that happened and she cried out in pain, I would probably cry myself. Even worse, she could run into traffic and get hit—or just get up and run away down the sidewalk. Having learned later about police in Egypt shooting dogs, I can only imagine how those nearby officers might have reacted if this dog howled and bit me because I had accidentally hurt or scared her.

As I gently stroked the dog's belly my mind turned to my two dogs back home. E-Style and Chewie, better known to friends and family as The Hogs. E-Style is my soulmate, she would have been almost 9 years old at the time. A little hairless, slate-colored, one-eyed Chinese Crested. Completely full of spunk and personality. Incredibly sweet and loving but still a little shit in her own way.

Chewie is my mom's dog. A little white male Chinese Crested mix that was approaching 5 years old at the time. Their personalities couldn't be more different. He's always been a sad little guy, sort of moping around and just looking depressed. E needs to know where you are at all times and be in that place with you but Chew is content to go in another room by himself and lay perched on top of the couch like a lethargic gargoyle. E loves laying on the sidewalk and baking in the sun, Mr. Chewpants loves the recliner and air-conditioning. E loves toys so much that she has a hand puppet alligator named Mr. Hat that she humps all over the house with regularity. Mr. Chew just wants to lay around and bite on his feet. Two vastly different dogs, supposedly of the same breed, but they are inseparable. My life revolves around the Hogs and they are never far from my thoughts.

I started to worry that maybe this Egyptian street dog had a disease or sickness that I could carry home somehow. I'd never forgive myself for that. Obviously, that's not really possible but my emotions were running wild and I was finding it harder to process everything clearly. There were so many things racing through my mind it was hard to latch onto one specifically and just take in the moment. With persistence, planning, and a little luck, I was able to break through the terrible circumstances to establish a relationship with this helpless little creature. I needed to appreciate what was happening rather than worry about my dogs on the other side of the world.

Simultaneously overcome with both peace and sadness, I felt like I must be the only person in the world to connect with that dog. To care for her, show her kindness, give her a soft caress. I had to be the first person to show an interest in her well-being. To acknowledge she was a living thing that deserved respect and a chance to survive in that brutal environment with its sadistic inhabitants. When she was in need of a hero to rescue her from the violence she endured on a daily basis, somehow, I found the strength within myself to step up and take whatever risk was necessary to save her. Ignoring my better judgment that told me only trouble and agony would be found if I pursued this, I followed through anyway because the dog needed me.

That's how I felt at that moment. It was an honor accompanied by an overwhelming sorrow. A feeling of immense pride, sincere gratitude, and incredible heartbreak. Each passing second became more of a challenge to fight back tears. I did not want to cry while petting the stray dog. Not there. Not on those streets in front of those people. I would not let them see I was broken because their cold-hearted, merciless attitude towards animals had made me get too involved for my own good. This damaged little girl laying on her back in the dirt needed me. She needed me to be strong for her and to show her what love is rather than get caught up in my own emotions. I had to push it back down deep inside, there would be time for it later.

The idea of calling an animal shelter never crossed my mind. If I had learned anything while in Cairo it was that animals were not a priority. Not just an assumption, I had been outright told that by the young woman I had talked to a few minutes earlier. I had no reason to believe animal shelters even existed in Egypt and I wouldn't have even known where to look for that kind of information. I didn't have a smart phone in 2010 and, even if I had internet access, by this time it was too late.

As I looked down at the nameless baladi dog I had stalked for two days, the inevitability of what I had to do next creeped into my thoughts. I had to leave. I had no idea how long I had been down there but surely it was too long. It had been a little before dusk when I went down there but by this point it was fully into the night. We had spent the last day and a half waiting to go and now it was time.

My stomach sank and my legs turned to jelly. My throat tightened up and my eyes started to get blurry. I had to force myself to stand up. There couldn't be any thinking about it and psyching myself out, I had to just do it. I gave the dog one last little rub on the chest. She had her eyes closed in total relaxation.

In one swift motion I stood up and started walking away. For whatever reason, I made the mistake of glancing back. She turned her head in my direction to see where I had gone then started to get up. With her tail wagging, she started trailing me. I had to move.

Making my way across the sidewalk, I looked up and noticed a couple sitting on a bench. The man had his arm around the woman and he yelled out to me.

"Why don't you take him in your hotel with you?" followed by a little chuckle between the two of them, clearly mocking me.

I stopped and sort of barked back at them, "Why don't you take her home with you?" It was the worst comeback of all time but I had nothing else.

"Ha!" He almost doubled over. I guess he felt the need to make fun of some tourist trying to help one of Cairo's worthless baladi dogs to feel better about his own shitty life. In a city full of assholes, he needed to make sure his lady knew that he was the King Asshole of Haram Street. That bench was his throne and I was his court jester. She must have been so impressed.

For a second, I considered striking up an actual conversation with him. Maybe I could convince him to help me or do the right thing by helping the dog. As he continued laughing, the thought faded almost as quickly as it had formed. He made a waving motion with his hand as if to say 'move along' then turned his attention back to the woman. Out of all the rude and heartless people I had encountered, this was the one man I wanted to punch in the face. The night had been painful enough without some blowhard trying to rub salt in the wound. Feeling vulnerable already, it just hit me the wrong way. If he had delivered a "welcome to Egypt" I probably would have snapped. His antics led me to assume his life was one of such great disappointment that he felt compelled to ridicule somebody for taking an interest in a street dog. I held onto that thought and just let it all slide. He wasn't worth it.

Since I had been standing there for a few seconds the dog nearly caught up to me. I turned my head around to see her hobbling along, tail swaying from side to side. It was like she was a normal dog and I was taking her for a walk. She looked so content, like she must have been thinking, "where are we going next?" It would have been cute if it weren't so tragic.

My heart started pounding again. I had to get away from her. She couldn't still be anywhere around me when I got near the hotel entrance. I didn't know what I would do if I had to shut the door in her face and I didn't know what the hotel staff would do if there were a mangled mutt just hanging around outside. I didn't want to find out.

I faced forward and started walking faster. I had to put some space between us quickly before it was too late. I felt like an Olympic power walker trying to jog while still walking. I should have just went for it and ran. Full dramatic effect would have been achieved and it wouldn't have allowed me to look back again. Unfortunately for me, I hadn't been using my best judgment the last few days, so once I stepped down off the sidewalk onto the access road I turned back to look one final time. It would be my undoing.

The dog stood still in the darkness. Staring blankly at me from the distance I had just created. Her tail was down. Her front right leg dangled slightly above the ground. She knew I was getting away from her and she could no longer catch me. I could see it in her eyes. My soul shattered.

To me, in that moment, we were of one mind. We were seeing each other for the last time and both of our hearts broke in unison. Our little love affair was over. I gave her everything I could in the short time allowed and we both had to accept it. I took a long look at her then did the hardest thing I had ever done in my life. I turned around, put my head down, and got into the hotel as fast as I could.

I sprinted through the lobby, looking at no one. I didn't want to make eye contact with anyone at the desk. Maybe they had seen what was going on outside, maybe they hadn't. I wanted to disappear. By the time I got on the elevator, my throat felt like I had a watermelon stuck in it. When the door opened on the fifth floor, I ran down the hall to our room. As I burst through the door, David was standing nearby. He touched me on the shoulder and opened his mouth to speak. I don't know if he got anything out before I dashed into the bathroom and closed the door behind.

I sobbed uncontrollably. Two day's worth of total frustration came out all at once. I cried like somebody had just died. Like a newborn bawling its way out into the world. I couldn't stop. I felt incredibly guilty. Not only had my escapades with the dog potentially ruined the last two days for David and Megan, now they had to listen to me weeping because of it. They would have been totally justified in smacking me with a big "I told you so" but these were my best friends. I'm sure it lurked somewhere in their subconsciouses and I wouldn't fault them for it.

After a few minutes I tried to calm down and straighten myself up. This was the inescapable ending. I had known that all along. We were about to get out of this place and I had to get my shit together. For David and Megan's sake, for the sake of getting out of the hotel without drawing attention, and ultimately for my own sense of well-being, I had to come to my senses and lock it all away.

We gathered up our things and made our way downstairs. The concierge called a taxi to take us to the airport. We didn't have to wait long before it arrived and we headed outside. I made it a point to not look down the sidewalk in the direction I had last seen the dog. I couldn't take seeing her again and I really couldn't take the idea of her seeing me again. She would get her hopes up only to have them crushed once more as we pulled away. She'd suffered enough.

## Chapter 7

I don't remember anyone speaking the entire hour-long ride to the airport. We arrived earlier than anticipated so we sat around the lobby a little while before going through security. Sometime during this period, we finally started talking again.

We went through at least five different security checks. Every twenty feet somebody wanted to see our passports. At one of the checks, David and I got singled out due to how different we looked from our pictures. We got our passports together in the fall of 2004. I was 22 years old, had long curly hair, and was relatively clean shaven. In 2010, I was 28, had much shorter hair with a receding hairline, and a full beard, which was described as "looking Egyptian" by the beardless camel scammer at the Pyramids. David would have been 20 in his first passport photo, with shaggy hair and a long, pointed goatee. In 2010, he had very short, clean cut hair, and almost no facial hair at all. We did look quite different, but 6 years had passed. Who in the world keeps the exact same look their entire life?

A security agent looked at my picture and cracked a smile. "This is you? What happened?" He was undeniably amused at my progression over the years. As any balding man could tell you, once certain people blessed with thick hair start noticing your hair loss they'll remind you of it any chance they get and never pass an opportunity to wisecrack at your expense. Despite all of their jokes being the most rehashed, unoriginal failures you've ever heard, making you feel sorry for their lack of comedic skills, you eventually get a little annoyed at hearing the same thing over and over again. Everybody starts to sound like your drunk uncle that keeps repeating himself.

Typically, I couldn't care less about this stuff but, like the guy on the bench a couple of hours earlier, this security guy irritated me more than usual because of the emotional strain I had been under. I had a lot of smart ass things I wanted to respond with, all battling to come out first.

"There are stray animals being openly abused in your streets. What happened? I just spent the last two days in your country on what was supposed to be a dream vacation stressing out over this emaciated dog that was being beaten by kids right in front of their parents and nobody gave a shit. What happened? I will drive over him without drive over him. What happened? Welcome to Egypt. What happened?"

I didn't really say any of those things. Good judgment would thwart my reactionary instincts this time. The security agent had something else in common with King Asshole of Haram Street: he also wasn't worth me doing something stupid. I was positive I would never come back to Egypt but there was no need to cause a scene at an airport.The flight was rough for me and the twelve hours to New York felt like an eternity. All I could think about was the dog and the way she looked at me the last time before I walked away. Once the plane took off there was a cold finality to everything. In my mind, the dog dropped dead the second we were in the air because I was her only hope and I had abandoned her with no chance of going back.

She was on the streets to fend for herself once again with no protector. I left my heart in a patch of dirt on the sidewalk in front of Haram Street.

Almost all I remember about that flight was feeling horrible. The only reprieve came early on in the form of the bizarre behavior of an old man sitting across the aisle. Before and during takeoff, he went through this cycle of looking straight ahead at the back of the seat in front of him for a few seconds, then violently jerking his head to the left to look out the window. It was as if he saw something in his peripheral vision and had to instantly look out of fear that it might be like that William Shatner episode of the Twilight Zone where the little gremlin was tearing at the wing of the plane. He must have repeated this for at least 15 minutes, looking forward then to the left a few seconds later. Somehow, the person next to him never reacted to it.

Despite how bad I felt, I couldn't help but laugh at the old man's antics. The longer it went on the harder it got to not erupt right there in the seat across from him. It was like those times when you get so exhausted or upset that every little thing is getting on your last nerve, but then randomly there's that one thing that comes out of nowhere to make you laugh so you just embrace it. I have no doubt that I would have still found this funny at any other point in my life under less strenuous circumstances, but my mental state on that plane was so low that I really needed something to lighten the load of the burden I was carrying. That old man might have saved me from a total breakdown with his little performance piece. David and I eventually started impersonating him but since we were sitting to his right he never noticed, too busy going hard left.

That episode with the old man has always stood out in my memory because it was all I had to distract myself from thinking about the dog. I'm sure I attempted to read or watch something, and in all honesty, I'm sure I did do those things, I just don't recall any specifics. Reading or watching a movie would require concentration and focus, two things I did not have. There was no room for anything else in my brain other than the little dog I left behind. The old man was a real-life improv comedy show happening two feet away. It was unavoidable. It was a distraction, and a sorely needed one at that.

At some point during the flight, Megan made the comment that there was nothing I could have done, that they would have never let me take the dog on the plane the way she was. I knew it was true. Even if I had the time to go out and buy a crate, there were too many other things that would have prevented the dog from being allowed to fly back home with me. She had no paperwork, no vaccinations, was severely underweight, had obvious injuries that hadn't been taken care of, and she would have probably gone insane being shut in a crate like that. I didn't have any record of her flying over with me so they would easily see that she was just a street dog I had found. A little baladi for which they would have no sympathy. I don't know that me telling the stories of getting her out from under the car one day and then feeding her the next would have been enough to convince authorities to let her board. I just had no idea of anything.

*Baladi*

Megan was trying to console me that I had done everything in my power for the dog and in the end it was just out of my hands, but to me nothing was ever going to make it right. With enough time passing the pain would dull, but I would never forget and I would never want to forget. If I didn't remember that dog then who else would? I was the only person in the world to ever connect with her and I had left her to die. I would never know what happened to her and I would never be at peace with it.

## Chapter 8

After a 12-hour red-eye flight, we landed in New York for a layover. My girlfriend Randi would be picking us up in Nashville a few hours later, so I called her to update her on our progress. After two weeks of little communication between us, I barely told her anything about the amazing trip we had just taken or the things we had seen. I spoke almost exclusively of the dog.

Aside from David and Megan, no one knew the events of the last 48 hours, so I was bursting to get it all out to somebody else. I needed the opinion of someone with a fresh perspective that wasn't tainted by the apparent Egyptian culture of animal cruelty. She was very supportive of my thinking: going down to stop the kids from chasing the dog, feeding it, getting close to it. She was sympathetic of my soft heart and how much the entire thing pained me on a personal level. She was also nervous about what it would mean going forward.

Once we got home to Bowling Green, Randi and I drove over to Mom's house to see the Hogs and look at pictures from the trip. There's nothing in the world like being greeted by dogs that have missed you. E-Style dancing around on her back feet, Chewie trotting around making his little pitiful high pitch squeaks; I lived for that and they never disappointed.

I briefly showed them both the highlights of places that they would recognize but skipped past everything else. I had to get to the pictures of the dog and tell Mom all about it. Randi leaned in to finally see the thing that had captivated me so intensely. It didn't take long before Mom's eyes started to well up. When I showed them video I took of her stumbling around the sidewalk and swinging her messed up leg around, I had to fight back crying again. It was the first time I had watched it myself, and it all came rushing back.

All it took was me getting upset to get Mom upset. I wouldn't personally know what it's like to see your child cry, but I can imagine it's difficult to watch—especially when that child is a 28-year-old man. I told Mom the same line I had repeated to David, Megan, and Randi, that I felt like I was the only person in the world to connect with the dog and I didn't know how I was supposed to go on with that.

The next day, I went back to work and everyone wanted to know all about my trip. Questions about all the historical places we had seen, what the food was like, what was my favorite thing, all of the usual. Once again, it all came back to the dog. I just couldn't let it go and everyone had to know about it. I got the same reaction from my coworkers as I had gotten from everyone else--I was bringing them down by constantly focusing on some trivial and unfortunate part of what was otherwise an incredible tour around Europe.

They didn't know what my objective was and I wasn't even sure myself. I just knew I couldn't let her be forgotten. Since no one in Egypt would notice or remember her, I had to make sure she didn't just disappear. She existed and she mattered and people had to know.On my lunch break, I called the local humane society for advice. The person I talked to told me, "We have plenty of dogs here that need homes. If you really want a dog, we have a lot and we get more every day."

I felt guilty but I wasn't going to be swayed. I couldn't.

We had a little bit of a back and forth about why I was doing this before I finally gave them the answer they needed to hear. "It's like when somebody comes in to adopt a dog from you, they lock eyes with one and, out of nowhere, it's obvious that that's the one that's supposed to go home with them. Somehow they just know. That's their dog. It was just waiting on them to come get it. That's what happened to me. That's my dog over there and I need help bringing her home."

Saying those words made it sink in with the person on the phone and for the first time it really all made sense to me. That was my dog in Cairo.

I was told to contact the Humane Society of the United States and they could possibly provide more information. After again explaining how personal the situation was to me, they took my information down to pass along to Humane Society International and said they would be in touch if they found anything.

It was a start and I was grateful. I was also getting more stressed out by the minute. This was Monday morning; factoring in the time difference it was close to 48 hours from when I had last actually seen the dog. The scope of what I was trying to do was daunting and the assumptions I was making about everything were countless. Sure, the dog came to the hotel multiple times the last two days I had been there but there was no guarantee she would continue doing that. With all the abuse she absorbed with each visit, it stands to reason that eventually she would either move on or take enough damage she might not recover. With her penchant for laying under cars and the drivers' willingness to "drive over him without drive over him" she could have easily been dead within the hour I left her. I had also drawn attention to her that she hadn't previously been given. I couldn't just take for granted that those officers stationed outside the HUSA would help her out again if necessary. With how spiteful everyone seemed, it's highly likely that me caring about the dog could have had the opposite effect on everyone that had seen our interactions. The urgency of everything made me feel like I might have an anxiety attack. I had to stay optimistic if the dog was going to have a chance.

That night after work, while feeling completely desperate, I took to YouTube and uploaded the video I had taken while down on the street. The title was "Stray Dog in Cairo, Please Help," with a description of everything that had happened. It was a long-shot, but I was willing to try anything.

Sleep that night was nonexistent. The bed was like hot concrete. The sheets were the underside of a car. The white noise of the box fan across the room was the never-ending honking of horns in the eternal Cairo traffic jam. Where was my sweet, street dog? Was she being chased and beaten by little brats? Was somebody feeding her? Did somebody "drive over her without drive over her?" I couldn't stop thinking about her and I felt more connected to her than ever, now that my mind was set on rescuing her.

Unbeknownst to me, my mom had told my brother about the dog and how upset I was. My older brother, Smitty, was living in northern Virginia at the time so I hadn't seen or talked to him yet, but that hadn't stopped Mom. She had told him I was panicking and she didn't know what to do. Tuesday afternoon, while I was at work, he called me with a potential lead.

He'd found a blog called One Fleeting Glimpse, that was written by an American woman named Iman Satori who had moved to Cairo. She brought her dog with her and adopted an Egyptian dog from a shelter called ESMA: The Egyptian Society for Mercy to Animals. The contact page on ESMA's website listed a woman named Kristen Stilt as the person to call in the U.S.A. This looked too good to be true. There was an animal shelter there the whole time and I had no idea.

I called Kristen and left a message explaining everything and it didn't take long for her to call me back. She was remarkably calm about the situation and eager to help. I was almost in shock. Could it be this easy? She asked me to send her an email with everything I could think of, the hotel address, pictures of the dog, description of the injuries, the times of day I saw her, anything else that would be useful, and she'd pass it along to Mona Khalil.

About thirty minutes after I emailed Kristen, I was copied in an email from the Humane Society of the United States to the Humane Society International about my situation. A couple of hours later, I received another email saying HSI had contacted an associate in Egypt and they were going to look into my case. Not long after, I got an email from Mona telling me they would move first thing the next morning to look for the dog and that they would keep going back until they found her.

As soon as I woke up Wednesday, I checked my email and found a message from Mona Khalil. "We got the girl. First inspection: front and back right leg injury, seems to be a hard car accident. Will be taken for x-ray tomorrow morning because none of the facilities we rent is working now. Also some problem with the mouth. She is safe now, comfortable, getting a full meal of chicken, rice, carrots and soup. Has her own room, bed and blanket. More info tomorrow. Love, Mona"

I was in tears. Unbelievable. Just like that, this little dog that was carrying around a piece of my heart on the other side of the world was safe. Never to be beaten, kicked, hungry, chased, or abused in anyway ever again. I was overcome with emotion. To be totally honest, I was never actually sure it was possible. I had no expectations that this would really work out. All I had was hope. It turned out that was enough.

## Chapter 9

Mona contacted me later that night with more details about the dog's condition. Both right legs had obvious injuries but the front was more severe. They also suspected something was wrong with her jaw. That was new to me.

I wondered what she had been through in the three and a half days since I was with her. Maybe she was more trusting of people and it had caused her to be tormented easier. Maybe she was still hanging around waiting for me. Maybe... I didn't even want to entertain the thought, but maybe it wasn't the same dog.

I needed to get them to send me a picture as soon as possible. Getting any dog off those streets would obviously be a good thing but I needed it to be my dog. I could only imagine having to break the news that this was a different dog and I needed them to go back out and search more. That would be a nightmare. All those thoughts would have to wait. It was too exciting to consider the "what ifs" and get pessimistic. They had a dog. They had my dog. It had to be.

Mona emailed me one more time with a suggestion: "We name the dog Nagat. It is an Arabic name that translates roughly to something like survivor or salvation. If you like it we will give it to her."

I liked it and it was highly appropriate, but I confess I didn't love it. Mona had every right to name the dog after everything she had done. Nagat was a beautiful name with great meaning, but I wanted to think on it for a while. This was my new nameless dog. I hadn't gotten a new dog in almost a decade.

When I got E-Style as a 19 year-old, I had her name saved in my back pocket waiting to use for years. E-Style. Dog E-Style. Say it out loud. I was a teenager when I came up with it and a teenager when I gave it to her. It was juvenile, but clever. Coming up with a new name was a big deal. I had to come up with something I would love. In all this time, I hadn't once thought to consider possible names. The entire process had been all about taking things one day at a time so as to not get ahead of myself in the event it didn't work out.

I got another email from Mona the next day after they took Nagat in for an x-ray. The front leg had an old fracture that had healed on its own. That was the small bulge I had seen on the street. She was also showing signs of imbalance and mild loss of coordination. They believed it was from either head trauma or vestibular disease. Unfortunately, it wasn't possible to have the CT scans done that would have answered a lot of these questions.

What I saw Nagat going through must have been a cakewalk compared to her past experiences. I had chalked up the stumbling around purely to the injured legs. I didn't even want to think about her getting hit so hard that she had head trauma. Mild loss of coordination? I couldn't even fathom what that would mean in the long run. And vestibular disease? I didn't have a clue what it was, but the word scared me. I was worried I may have gotten in over my head.

The good news in the email was that she was eating well and I would be getting pictures soon. I still had concerns that maybe it wasn't the same dog and the pictures would put that to rest. If it was the same dog, I would be ecstatic to see her again and in a good environment. I didn't know what ESMA looked like, but anything was better than sleeping under cars on Haram Street. I never thought I'd see her sweet, sad eyes again. If it wasn't, well… at least a dog in poor condition was going to get help and we'd address what to do later.

Mona then said something that has always stuck with me, "I sure hope you can get this girl out pending on one thing, there is no way I will send this girl to the USA to then hear vets there recommend putting her down. She either is saved to go live safely and happily in a family or she lives with us here and we will do our best for her as much as we can. Even if her adoption possibilities are limited or none. Please try to understand me on this matter. I am not pro-humane euthanasia for such cases at all."

It told me a lot about her and ESMA that this new dog they had just taken in with potentially lifelong serious health concerns would never be in danger of being put down. I couldn't imagine how they were able to sustain that ideology with however many animals they must have, but it was refreshing and impressive. I think Mona was trying to put a little fear in me about how seriously they take caring for their animals; if I wasn't up for it, then they wouldn't even consider sending Nagat to me. It made me wonder what kind of issues they have had with adopters or fosters and how common it was to send animals out of the country only to find out the new owners had put them down or given them up again.

Eventually, I came up with a potential name. I didn't want to explain why I chose it because I didn't want Mona to think I was making fun of the Egyptian accent, but I felt compelled to go ahead with the name suggestion.

Sphynx.

It seems generic on paper, but it was to be pronounced "sfeenkus" like the way we heard a lot Egyptians said Sphinx. I don't know why I changed the 'i' to a 'y' in the spelling. I'm not going to act like it was intentional. I was probably thinking about the sphynx cat breed and confused the spelling. The name was funny to me, a little inside joke representing one of the very few things I enjoyed about Cairo. I'm the guy that named his dog E-Style. It's just my sense of humor.

When I pitched it to Mona, I spelled it "Sphynx" in the email and didn't tell her how I planned to pronounce it. Except for the very first email that was sent to Kristen and me both, she was ending everything with a very formal "regards." I didn't want to cross any lines.

Mona immediately rejected it. She said it was a male name and if I liked more pharaonic names then she could make some suggestions and we would have to speak more on this later. Like I said before, I liked Nagat for its meaning and the fact that it's a legitimate Arabic word, but once I came up with Sphynx (sfeenkus) it was too hilarious to let go.

I decided that the next time we spoke of it I would spell it Sphyncus, more like how it sounds out loud. It still looks like Sphynx, but is clearly not. It has the "cus" to make sure you get that second syllable. Sphyncus. I liked it. I just had to convince Mona.

The next day, I got a message on Facebook that made my jaw drop. It was from Iman Satori, the woman that ran the One Fleeting Glimpse blog. ESMA had posted my video of Sphyncus down on the street with a brief explanation of the story, saying they needed a flight parent. Iman was flying back to Evansville, Indiana in a month and was offering to be the flight parent. She even had an extra dog crate that was airline approved. What were the odds? She was essentially the person that started it all. Without Iman I don't know that Smitty would have learned of ESMA, and I don't know that I would have found them either. The coincidence was just insane. The real sweetener to it was Evansville is only two hours from Bowling Green. The universe was sympathetic to my plight; it wanted me to have this dog.

Iman was also able to give me a rough estimate of what flying Sphyncus over might cost. She flew her Rottweiler to Egypt two years earlier for $750. That's a lot of money when you're broke, but at least it gave me a goal. I decided to do some online crowdfunding and went with the now defunct site ChipIn. I chose it over Kickstarter because you would receive the money whether or not your goal was met, and you got the money as soon as it was donated. I launched the ChipIn campaign that very same day. Within an hour, I had my first donation--$10 from a friend. Then... nothing.

I refreshed my ChipIn page relentlessly that first day. It was just as barren and disappointing every time. Just when I was starting to feel discouraged, I got another email from Mona that also had a batch of pictures. I skipped right over her message and just started downloading the pictures. This was it. I was about to find out for sure if this was in fact the same dog I had fallen in love with.

Before opening the first picture, I stopped myself. They had invested a lot in this dog. Serious time, effort, and work went into not only retrieving her but also inspecting her and caring for her. They dealt with my constant nagging. They were getting things prepared to send her over. If I opened the pictures and saw a different dog there, I still had to adopt it. I couldn't just abandon everything. It wouldn't be right. I would tell them it wasn't the same dog and see if they could go looking again for mine, but at this point, a week had passed. All hope wouldn't necessarily be gone, but the chances of them finding my dog would be significantly slimmer. If they did find her then I would have to adopt them both. If not, I had to resign myself to saving this one. It was a lot processing to do, but I had to steel myself up just in case.

I opened the first picture.

Sitting cross-legged outside on a tiled floor was who I presumed to be Mona Khalil. A lovely looking Egyptian woman with a big smile on her face. Sitting in her lap and being held in her arms was my little street dog. My dirty, injured, stinky, sweet little girl. She had her tongue hanging out and looked like she was smiling. The piece of my heart that I thought I had lost. Seeing her again, knowing it was her, seeing her being held and loved, I just broke down crying. We did it. We really did it.

She looked so happy in all the pictures. Standing there smiling at the camera in each of them, it was like a totally different dog. Just a week after describing her as the most pitiful thing I had ever seen, she was already enjoying life. She was trusting people. I must have flipped through those pictures a dozen times before even looking at Mona's message.

The email itself was full of good news. Mona described Sphyncus' behavior as a total sweetheart. She greeted the workers each day with licking, tail wagging, and body wiggling. She was given her first combined vaccine, would be getting her rabies shot in a few days, and would receive her boosted vaccine in three weeks.

I checked back on my ChipIn later that night to find I had another $100. It was from my brother. We fought like all siblings do growing up, but Smitty has always been a hero to me when I needed him. He has never shied away from helping me out and this was the perfect example. Seeing my little money raising campaign sitting there with $10 in it must have looked pathetic to anyone that saw it, so he boosted me up. I don't know if he's ever been fully appreciated or recognized for the role he played in this rescue mission, but he was vital. Without his help who knows how it would have played out?

Two days later, I got a few more pictures from Mona. Sphyncus was rolling around on the ground trying to play with other dogs. She just looked so happy. One of the other dogs in the pictures was Mona's, a sweet looking fellow named Antar. I always referred to E-Style as the love of my life and that was Antar to Mona. He was described to me as "the love or best friend of all the shelter dogs." It made me feel good to know that as I was developing this new friendship with Mona, she had Antar there watching over Sphyncus.

A few days after the second batch of pictures, I got a troubling message from Mona. Delta had enacted an embargo on flying animals in the summer due to the heat. Iman was already booked on a Delta flight so she was eliminated as the flight parent. She did, however, offer to sell me her extra crate and leave it at the ESMA shelter for whenever we found a way to get Sphyncus over.

The TV station I work for decided to run a story about everything as an attempt to help with the fundraising. Although it did result in a few more people contributing money, I also got some flack from our viewers saying "why don't you just adopt a dog here in America?" That old song and dance again. There was a bit of irony to it because Bowling Green is home to a huge resettlement agency that assists refugees coming to America and here I was trying to bring over what was essentially a refugee dog, but was being told it was a waste of time.

There was one really funny part to it, though. When we got back from the trip, I randomly cut my hair into a mohawk. I wanted to keep my "Egyptian looking" beard so I left the sides of my hair a little grown out to blend into it. Not my best look and I really have no idea why I did it. The day the interview was shot, I was already at work and wasn't given any notice beforehand. I was dressed in my usual t-shirt and cut off shorts. Real classy, but it gets better. It wasn't just any shirt, it was my Radiohead shirt from the 2008 In Rainbows tour with the song lyrics "You'll go to hell for what your dirty mind is thinking." Yes, I wore that to work. The real kicker is that due to the framing of the camera shot the only part you could read was "You'll go to hell" as I stood there with my mohawk and scruffy beard. I guess it was no surprise that viewers didn't flock to my cause. One of my co-workers will still occasionally bring it up, referring to it as my "go to hell shirt."

A few days later another unsung hero of this story stepped forward. My longtime friend and bandmate Michael Farmer was a contributing writer for Louisville's Velocity website under his alter ego Kentucky Prophet. He did a piece on what was becoming known amongst friends as "The Sphyncus Story."

For those not in the know, Louisville is a much bigger and more progressive city than Bowling Green. Most anyone in Kentucky would say Louisville has its own identity almost completely separate from the rest of the state. When the story went live, I started getting messages from readers almost instantly. It was being shared on other sites and reaching more people; everyone wanted updates on where things stood. The most incredible part is my ChipIn campaign was actually overfunded within a couple days. I even had people from overseas throwing in money.

Much like Smitty, most people probably don't know how important of a part Mike played in all this, but it was huge. He might have just written one single piece on a website but it single-handedly took care of all of my remaining financial issues. Less than three weeks had passed between when I started fundraising and completed it. Sphyncus was coming home.

## Chapter 10

In the back of my mind I always wondered if Mona took me seriously when I first said I wanted to bring Sphyncus to the USA. ESMA gets a lot of requests from people to take in animals that they find. The person initially promises to help out and give money but ultimately most just disappear, leaving the shelter scrambling to pay for another mouth to feed. Somewhere in the back of her mind she had to consider that I may be another one of them.

I knew it was a bizarre request from the beginning when I told ESMA that I was an American tourist who was only around a street dog a couple times before just leaving her there with no attempt to find help. Mona described looking for a specific dog on Haram Street as "asking us to find a certain fish from the ocean." A proverbial needle in a haystack. Even though Mona and ESMA had done the truly hard work, she seemed very appreciative of me the longer it dragged on. She stopped ending her emails with "regards" and started saying things like "my friend." All the trials and tribulations we were coming across didn't discourage me at all and I assumed she respected me for not giving up on this dog I had bonded with. I don't really know for sure. What I do know is that Mona will always hold a special place in my heart for taking a chance on Sphyncus and me. We have a unique friendship based on circumstances that will most likely never be duplicated.

I stayed in touch with Iman and she gave me a lot of insight into the personality of baladi dogs, what to be

*Baladi*

aware of and ready for. Some of it sounded outright hilarious, but I got the feeling that Sphyncus was going to be a handful. As a former street dog, she would probably have wild dog not far down her bloodline, meaning she could be more territorial than a normal dog. Iman initially had adopted two baladis but one became aggressive toward the other and had to go back to ESMA. If Sphyncus became aggressive towards E and Chew I didn't know what I would do.

Iman's dog was smart, but destructive and hard to potty train. With E and Chew being nine and five years old, respectively, it had been a while since I had to potty train a dog.

The last thing she warned me about was that since they're street dogs, baladis are naturally scavengers. I could expect Sphyncus to possibly steal things and hide them. To be honest, I actually hoped she would because it sounded hilarious.

When E-Style was younger, she would take all her chew-bones and toys and hide them under my bed. I had a lot of storage totes under there, but at the foot there was an empty space of about 10 inches that ran across the entire width. That's where E would hide things. Sometimes she would even hide in there herself since the sheets hung down to where you could barely see her. That space was known as The Batcave and it was legendary the first few years of her life. The idea of having another dog that would hide things made me nostalgic for E's puppy days; I was eager for the chance to have something similar.

As June went on, we concluded that we weren't going to find a flight parent so Sphyncus would be

75

flying over alone, as cargo. Mona took the lead and started contacting various airlines. In an odd twist, it turned out Delta's embargo wasn't a "full embargo" but it was never explained to me what that meant. Apparently, it was possible Sphyncus could have flown over with Iman all along, but it was too late now.

After a couple of weeks with no news, on Thursday morning, July 8th, I got an email from Mona saying Sphyncus would be flying out of Cairo in three days via Lufthansa. As cargo, her crate was too big for Nashville so she'd be going to Atlanta instead. Her flight was at 4:30 a.m. Cairo time on Sunday which was 9:30 p.m. Saturday night in Bowling Green, and I wouldn't be able to pick her up until 9:00 a.m. Monday morning. 36 hours was a long time for a dog to be traveling like that. This little dog would spend more time in the air than most people I've known. She'd be traversing three continents. I felt like a proud dad.

The only thing left to do was transfer the money to ESMA. I headed over to a Western Union in a Kroger and I'll never forget the exchange for as long as I live.

"Hi, how can I help you?"

"I need to send some money over to Egypt."

The girl at the counter was immediately skeptical. "Okay. And how much will you be sending?"

"Eleven hundred dollars," I made sure to look as relaxed as I could. I knew how it sounded, I knew the reaction I would get.

"Eleve…" she trailed off and looked up at me.

"Yep."

"What's this for?"

"A dog."

"A dog?"

"Yes."

"And this is your dog?"

"Uh, yes. It will be."

"Why did you leave your dog in Egypt?"

"Well, that's a long story. It's a street dog that I found while I was over there and I couldn't bring her back with me so she's been at a shelter the last couple of months until we could work it out. There's more to it than that but, yeah, she's my dog. They're sending her over to me."

"Do you know these people? Are you sure this isn't some kind of scam?" I knew where she was going with this so I just went ahead and said it.

"No, this isn't some Nigerian prince asking me to send over a thousand dollars with my bank account number then he'll send me money back. This is a legit thing, I promise."

"Okay… but once it's sent over it's gone. I don't know that you could get it back."

"I don't want it back. I want my dog."

"Okay, well let me get somebody over here to help out with this." She got another person that I assumed could only be her supervisor and explained it to her. Now I had two skeptical women looking at me like I was about to get swindled and they were the last line of my defense. The icing on the cake came when they asked for the name I was sending it to. There was no possible way I could remember and pronounce the name Mona had given me in the email that morning. Pulling a folded-up piece of paper out of my pocket, I smirked as

I showed it to them: Mohamed Ahmed Abdl Khalek. They absolutely loved that.

"And you know this person?" the supervisor asked.

"Well, no. But I've been talking with another person at the animal shelter for almost two months. They have my dog. I trust them. This isn't a scam."

"And she told you that once you send this money then it's gone. It could be very difficult to get it back. You most likely wouldn't get it back."

"Yeah, that's fine. I'm not worried about it. I promise you, this is a real thing. I know how it looks. I know how it sounds. They're sending the dog in three days, I need to get this done. I don't need you to be comfortable with it, I just need you to do it."

I messaged Mona back once it was over and told her we were all squared away over here. I just had two final questions. Does she know her name and how do you actually pronounce Nagat? It turns out Sphyncus was not very familiar with the name Nagat. Mona said "she wags her tail and smiles to anything you call her so feel free to call her anything you want. She is a real love."

That settled it then. She would be Sphyncus. Sphyncus Nagat. Sphyncus the survivor.

At home, Randi was cautiously enthusiastic but this was one hundred percent my venture. I had never even asked her opinion on it. I didn't feel like there were any options; the dog had to be off the streets and she had to be with me. We never talked about the what ifs. I hadn't checked to see if it was okay with her. I just basically said, "I have to do this" and left it at that. She respected it, but wasn't exactly thrilled. She had two middle-aged cats in the apartment and was worried how they would adapt.

Did it make me a selfish asshole? Maybe. But this was bigger than me. It was the right thing to do. It was the only thing to do. Any time somebody questioned me or my motives, I told them all the same thing, "You weren't there. You didn't see what I saw. You didn't feel what I felt." It was a truth that's power couldn't be overstated.

Sunday afternoon, Randi and I packed up her car and headed down to Atlanta to stay the night. It's about a 4 and half hour drive from Bowling Green so we had a lot of time to talk about things and let it all sink in. Our entire lives were going to be different starting the next day. Sphyncus was still young so with any luck she would live a long time, we could have 15 years or more of this former hobo dog hanging out with us. I don't know how true it is that mixed breeds have less health issues but, if it were true, surely this baladi would be strong as an ox. She'd already survived getting hit by a car and taking countless blows from little bastards chasing her around, if that's not tough then I don't know what is. Soon she would be laughing in their faces from a big comfy bed in the cool air conditioning surrounded by food and toys. Sphyncus 1, Egypt 0.

## Chapter 11

The big day was here. It had been over eight weeks since I last saw Sphyncus standing there staring at me in the darkness as I practically ran away with tears in my eyes. She didn't even have a name then, and now she had two. I hoped she remembered me.

We arrived at the Atlanta airport cargo warehouse to check in and receive the papers to take to Border Control. The area I stood in was maybe ten feet by ten feet and surrounded by fencing. Sphyncus was in that warehouse somewhere and the anticipation was killing me. If I knew where to look I might have been able to see her in the crate.

Customs and Border Control wasn't too far away. I was immediately uncomfortable walking in. It felt like a doctor's office or somewhere you go to get drug tested. A very dull, sterile environment. Chairs to the left of the room, a help counter straight ahead and another to the right. Nothing else. I walked up to the counter that was across from the door. An older woman greeted me.

"Can I help you?" she asked with a very serious look.

I put the papers on the counter. "Yes, I'm here to pick up my dog. I just went by the warehouse and they gave me these to bring you before they'd release her to me."

Silence. She picked up the pages and thumbed through them. "Okay, Mr. Hines. Have a seat for just a few minutes."

We nervously sat down and I started to feel a little intimidated. Border Control was serious stuff. I thought maybe I was in over my head before, but now I knew that I was. Surely this sort of thing didn't have to happen every time somebody flew a dog over.

"Mr. Hines?"

"Yes?" I got up and approached the counter again.

"I just need to ask you a few things before I can let you be on your way."

"Sure thing."

"What is your address in Atlanta?"

"We don't live in Atlanta. We live in Kentucky. Bowling Green."

She tilted her head forward and looked over her glasses at me. "You don't live in Atlanta?"

"No," I answered. "We drove down about four and a half hours from Bowling Green. I was told they couldn't send my dog to a closer airport so she had to come here."

"So why does this list your address as being in Atlanta?"

"I have no idea. Can I see what it says?"

She held it up in front of me so I could see it but not hold it. I hadn't actually looked at the paperwork on the way over. The address made absolutely no sense.

Josh Hines
1960 Stonehenge Ave. Apt 1 Bowling
Atlanta, Georgia
USA

It took me a second to put it together but it made sense to some degree. The final destination for the crate was in Atlanta, there was no reason for Kentucky to be listed. Since there was no physical address that Sphyncus would be going to in Atlanta, my apartment address in Bowling Green was listed. It didn't make any sense to look at, but I wasn't really sure how it could've been done any differently.

"I think I see what happened here" I told her. "See, that's my address listed above Atlanta because that's the address I gave them, where I live in Bowling Green. See how it says Bowling above Atlanta? That doesn't make any sense. They probably just got confused and the printer cut off. Does that make sense to you?"

She stared at me blankly, not at all happy with my explanation. Defying all fashion sense, I was still sporting the mohawk and beard look. I could see this old woman applying every possible stereotype to me as I looked at her hoping she would just accept my logic regarding the address mix up.

"Mr. Hines, can I see your driver's license?" She was entering interrogation mode.

I pulled it out of my wallet and handed it over.

"What's this address?"

"Oh, that's my old address. I haven't gotten a new license since I moved." It was my parents' old address that I had moved out of a couple of years earlier.

"Well, it looks like we have a problem here. Is that your wife there?"

"No, that's my girlfriend. That's her address on the papers you have. I moved in with her a couple of years ago at that Stonehenge address."

The woman motioned for Randi to get up and come over to the counter. "Ma'am, can I see your driver's license? We've got a label for this crate that doesn't match Mr. Hines' driver's license and I need to see some sort of proof of where this animal is going."

Randi pulled her license out of her purse. She stared at it for a couple of seconds looking worried as she handed it over.

"Miss Hunton, what is this address?" My heart sank. This was not what needed to happen.

Randi replied, "That's my old address before I moved into our current apartment. I moved in the apartment in 2008 a few months before Josh moved in with me."

"This address isn't even the same city," the woman responded. I could see her getting more and more irritated by the second and every answer we gave was somehow more damning than what came before it.

"Yes, I lived in Munfordville for a year before moving back to Bowling Green. It's about 40 miles north. I was working in Elizabethtown for a year so I lived in Munfordville as a halfway point to make it easier on us." Randi was significantly calmer than I was and much more formal in her answers.

"Do either of you have anything proving that you live at this address? Maybe some mail?" I took that question as a positive that she was acknowledging the flub of our Bowling Green address being listed above Atlanta as an actual, real address.

Randi was quick to respond, "I think I have some mail in the car, let me go out and check."

Her car was always a total mess of junk, mail, water bottles, clothes, anything that could just be tossed aside. It frustrated me to no end, but suddenly I was thankful for it because I knew she would have mail in there. I stood at the counter hoping the woman would say something to break the tension but she gave me nothing. Silence. She looked incredibly impatient. It was one of the most awkward times I can recall in my life. The epitome of seriousness on one side of the counter, an idiot with a curly mohawk and beard wearing cut off shorts on the other.

Randi came hurrying back in with a handful of mail, flipping through it as she opened the door and made her way to the counter. "Shit," is all she said as she sat it down on the counter.

The woman started thumbing through it and let out an agitated sigh. "Now what is this address?" she asked. I didn't think it possible for her to sound more annoyed, but there she was.

"That's my P.O. Box" I said. "I've had my mail sent there for years so I would always have something permanent."

"This won't do" the woman told us. "We have a problem here. This is already mislabeled and now you can't show me any proof you actually live at this address. You have shown me three additional addresses. I have four addresses here." I could only imagine the horror that was written all over my face. What a mess we had created for ourselves simply by not keeping our driver's licenses up to date.

Everything that everyone had worked so hard to do the last couple of months was crashing down before my eyes. I knew there was nothing I could say that wouldn't be digging a deeper hole. I was sure the security agent could smell the fear on me.

"Let's start from the beginning," the agent said. "Explain what's going on with all of these addresses and why the shipping label says the dog is coming to Atlanta."

"Because the dog did come to Atlanta. She isn't being shipped to Kentucky."

"Why does the label say Atlanta?"

"How would I know that? I didn't go to Egypt and make the label myself. The shelter made it and I'm sure there was some confusion with how our cities and states work."

"What are all of these addresses? Where do you actually live?"

"I live at 1960 Stonehenge Avenue, Apartment 1. Bowling Green, KY. The one that's mostly written on the papers."

"So why does it say Atlanta?" she asked again. The classic tactic of trying to trip you up by repeating the same questions phrased slightly differently.

"You can see on the label it says 1960 Stonehenge Ave, Apt 1, Bowling above where it says Atlanta. You know that doesn't make any sense because there isn't a Bowling Atlanta. Look it up and see if that address exists. The Stonehenge address. I bet there's not one here. I don't know how the label ended up like that, but it's obvious it was meant to say Bowling Green,

Kentucky but the Green and Kentucky were left off. How else should it have been labeled?"

The woman wasn't interested in humoring my attempt to turn it around on her. "So tell me how you came across this dog."

"I was in Cairo. She was on the street in front of our hotel, emaciated and being abused. I felt sorry for her so I fed her and got attached to her. I had to do something. It's a long story but that's basically it."

"And how long were you in Egypt?"

"Three days."

"Three days?" she asked, pitching her voice higher.

"Yeah, just three days. It was part of a longer trip we took through Europe and Cairo is where it ended."

"How many times did you see this dog?"

"I saw her the last two days I was there and I interacted with her twice. The first time I stopped some kids from chasing her and hitting her. She went under a car and I got her out but she was scared and ran off. The next day I fed her and gave her water. That's when she warmed up to me and I was able to pet her. I was probably with her about an hour that time, I'm not really sure. You don't know what it's like over there. It's bad." I said, looking down and shaking my head.

"Why not just get a dog here?"

"I've been asked that a lot. My local Humane Society asked me that when I reached out to them for help. The Humane Society of the United States, Humane Society International, literally almost everyone has asked me that. You just had to be there. I guess I just connected with this dog and had to save her."

The woman blankly stared at me. No empathy at all. "What type of dog is this? Are you planning to breed this dog? Is she spayed?"

"She's a baladi," I said. The woman tilted her head slightly. I quickly clarified "a mutt. That's what they call them over there."

"Is the dog spayed, Mr. Hines?"

"No, she isn't spayed. They told me she was too underweight. When they picked her up, they concentrated on getting her healthy and vaccinated but she never put on much weight so they didn't feel comfortable spaying her. I have no plans to breed this dog or any dog at all ever. I'm going to have her spayed as soon as a vet here okays it."

The woman continued to stare at me blankly. "Not spayed," she repeated back to me.

I was starting to get annoyed, like she was accusing me of something but wouldn't come out with it.

"So, you went to Egypt for three days, saw this dog, and wanted to bring her here. To the United States." I wasn't sure if it was a question or just recapping it back at me so I could hear how ridiculous it sounded from the other side.

"Yes. It's a different world over there. I'm a big animal person. I've been a vegetarian since I was 20. There's a long story to this whole thing. It's taken almost two months to get her here from when I left."

The woman's blank stare was unwavering. "So, you're a big animal person but had to have this dog from another country shipped over here that you only saw a couple of times to a different state than you actually live in rather than just adopting a dog in Kentucky."

"Yes." That's all I could think to say.

"Who sent the dog over to you?"

"They're called ESMA. It's an acronym for Egyptian Society for Mercy to Animals. As far as I know, they're the only animal shelter in Cairo. The only one I could find."

"So you what? Called them and they came to your hotel and got the dog?"

"No, no. I didn't talk to them until after I got home. The time when I was feeding her and able to pet her was right before I left. I didn't have time to contact anyone because we had to catch our flight. I had to leave the dog there. It was awful. I didn't know what to do. I made some calls to the Humane Society when I got home and my brother is actually the one that found the ESMA shelter online. There's a long story to all of that, too." The woman was not even slightly interested in my story.

"So you never even met these people that sent the dog over?"

"No, they've had her for almost two months. I've been in constant contact with them the entire time. I sent them money and everything, they're trustworthy."

"They're trustworthy but you never met them? You don't actually know them." Again, I didn't know if this was a question or a statement meant to make me see the absurdity of my story.

"Not personally, no. Only online. I've been talking with them for the last two months."

At that, the woman shifted her weight in a yet another display of annoyance and disbelief that she clearly wanted me to pick up on. "So you don't know the people that shipped this dog over?"

"No."

"And are you sure that this is the same dog?"

"Yes."

"And how do you know that?"

"You know, at first I was actually skeptical of that myself but they sent me a lot pictures. It's the same dog. She has some injuries that they described that perfectly matched what I saw. I have no doubt it's the same dog, as crazy as everything must sound."

"Have the injuries been taken care of? What types of injuries are we talking about?"

"She has a fracture in her front leg that healed on it's own. She had a limp when I saw her. They think something might be wrong neurologically, like she's off balance sometimes. Their vet said he thinks it most likely came from being hit by a car. She has some hair spots missing on her legs. Almost like cigarette burns or something." I was thinking surely that would soften this woman up some. Who wouldn't have sympathy for a dog hit by a car with possible cigarette burns on her? A Border Control officer apparently wouldn't.

"So we have an injured dog that hasn't been spayed being shipped over by people you've never met from another country."

"...yes. You have all of her paperwork there. You can see she doesn't have any health concerns or she would have never been allowed on a plane over here in the first place. She's fully vaccinated and everything."

"You do realize that if they smuggled something in this dog that it will fall on you?"

"What?" I was shocked by the question.

"If they smuggled something in this dog, whether you know about it or not, that will come down on you." It came across like she was tired of beating around the bush and finally said what she had been wanting to say the entire time.

"Well, I don't know of anything being smuggled so it wouldn't make any sense to do that. They're an animal shelter. I don't know of any reason why that would happen."

"Mr. Hines, I don't care if you know about it or not. People that you have never personally met sent over a live animal from Egypt to the United States. To a state you don't even live in with an address on the label that you can't prove you live at. This dog is your responsibility now and if something has been smuggled in it that falls on you."

Now it was my turn to stare back blankly. My mouth was slightly open and I could feel my eyes starting to water. I had no idea what to say. Technically everything she said was true but none of the insinuations had any merit. She was just straight up raking me over the coals and I had nothing left to respond with.

"Mr. Hines, please have a seat. I'm going make some calls." The woman pointed toward the chairs where Randi was sitting and walked away from the counter.

I felt sick. Like everything was in slow motion. Trying to retrace everything and figure out how this all went so badly, I kept seeing Sphyncus's eyes in the darkness staring at me as I turned away from her, reliving that scene over and over again. Everything I had done, everything ESMA and Mona had done, it was all unraveling. A domino effect all starting with a post office box from six years earlier and us being lazy about changing our driver's licenses. I was shaking in my chair.

Randi was trying to calm me down, but my mind was flooded with all the possibilities of what might happen next. I had read stories online about things going wrong with animal adoptions from overseas. When it was some sort of extreme scenario like this where the dog or cat had nowhere to go and it would take money or effort to place them somewhere, the word "destroyed" was often used when telling what became of the animal. Destroyed. Like an old building being torn down or a car being junked. Destroyed. A harsh word to use when referring to a living creature, but I became fixated on it. I could not let that happen.

As powerless as I felt, there was no way Sphyncus was getting shipped off to a high kill shelter in Atlanta to be destroyed. I couldn't even imagine some other asshole adopting her. She was my dog, goddamn it. We were bonded. This was meant to be. Too much had happened to set this up. Too many obstacles overcome. Too many coincidences to ignore. Too much hope and hard work. How could I go home without my dog? What would I tell Mona? How could I live with myself?

It felt like we sat in those chairs for an eternity. The entire two months leading up to this Border Control nightmare seemed to play out in real time in my head all over again. I was the most bush-league animal rescuer of all time. I tried to save a dog from the streets only to have it destroyed at an animal shelter two states away because I didn't update my driver's license. That would be my big story, the legacy of Sphyncus.

As I sat there with my head in my hands staring at the floor, I heard a voice calling to me. A completely new voice. "Mr. Hines?"

I looked up and turned my head toward the counter. It wasn't somebody new, it was the same grumpy old woman gearing up to deliver more bad news. My legs turned to jelly, just like when I had to get up from petting Sphyncus in Cairo. I didn't want to stand up and face what was coming.

"Mr. Hines?" the woman repeated.

"Yeah?" I stood up and walked over. Something was different about her. She had sort of a chipper demeanor.

"Mr. Hines, you can go pick up your dog now." Her eyes almost lit up behind her glasses and she smiled at me. "Take this and go back to the warehouse you went to before coming here. They'll have you sign a release form then escort you to your dog. You're free to go. Enjoy your new dog." The woman smiled again, a real honest to goodness smile. Leaving the papers on the counter, she turned to walk away.

I stood there for a second watching her, not knowing what to make of everything. There was no explanation, just the conclusion of the solo performance of good-cop-bad-cop. Just moments before I had made up my mind that this woman would be my sworn enemy until the end of my days, but now I wanted to jump over the counter and hug her.

Snatching up the papers from the counter, I turned to Randi and simply said, "let's go" while heading straight for the door. Out in the hot Atlanta summer air, I tried to piece together what could have led to our fortune reversing course so drastically.

The only thing that's ever made sense to me is that somebody was sent over to inspect Sphyncus during or after our questioning. They saw how scrawny and pitiful she was, and there was no way she could possibly be used for smuggling or breeding or whatever they were concerned about.

It was almost 10:30 A.M., two and a half hours from when we initially arrived at the airport. My heart was racing as we headed back over to the warehouse. Surely, there wasn't anything else that could stand in our way. I couldn't imagine how anything could possibly top what we had just gone through. Sphyncus was everything I told them she was and now she was mine.

I signed some papers in the warehouse office and the man escorted us through the fencing to a dog crate.

I couldn't speak. It was Sphyncus. She was curled up on a little brown blanket in the crate. It was really her, right in front of me.

The sound of our voices and footsteps must not have woken her up because when we lifted the crate there wasn't any sort of commotion inside indicating we had startled her. She didn't make a sound. There was a shipping label taped to the top and I saw my name on it above the jumbled address that had almost sent the whole thing off the rails. We went straight out to the parking lot and sat the crate down.

I crouched down to look in the door of the crate. Sphyncus stared out at me with her entire body wiggling like it was on a set of swivels. Her tail was a helicopter propeller. I poked my finger through the bars and she licked at it repeatedly. She was so happy.

Any doubts I ever had about this not being the same dog I had connected with on the streets were gone. After almost two months, we finally met again and the circumstances couldn't have been any different. The foreboding darkness was gone. The distance between us was gone. The sad eyes, gone. No kids to chase her. No cars to sleep under. No walking away this time.

I desperately wanted to let her out of the crate but I thought it best to leash her up in the car just in case she tried to run. She had waited 36 hours in there. It pained me to think it, but she could stand to wait a few minutes longer until we got somewhere suitable. It was obvious by the smell that she had messed in the crate numerous times, but how could she not? It must have seemed to her that she was now living in that crate.

There aren't words to describe what I felt. New friendships had been forged through the most coincidental circumstances on the internet, breaking down cultural barriers across an ocean for a common objective. Speed bumps popped up repeatedly, but we stayed the course, refusing to be denied. All challenges had been overcome. There was a goal and despite the odds being stacked against us, we achieved it. I had left a needle in a haystack on Haram Street and Mona Khalil went back to find it. In that moment, crouched down on the sidewalk under the hot sun in Atlanta, I looked at Sphyncus's eyes staring back at me and knew everything had been worth it.

This was my proudest accomplishment of my entire life.

## Chapter 12

As I sat on the ground sweet talking Sphyncus through the crate door, Randi pulled the car around to the sidewalk. It was clear the crate wasn't going to fit. We briefly considered one of us lifting the crate up to the open car door while the other was in the backseat on the opposite side to open it and coax Sphyncus out. We abandoned that idea because we didn't know how she would handle being unsecured in a moving vehicle. Leaving her in the crate was the best arrangement.

Randi's car was a 2007 Toyota Yaris. Not tiny but still small. Sphyncus didn't weigh a lot, I guessed around 20 pounds, but the crate was big and too awkward for one person to pick up. The new plan was to pick it up together, set the edge of the crate on the edge of the seat, and then try to shove it in, all while keeping Sphyncus calm inside. We got as far as setting the edge of the crate on the edge of the seat, but it wouldn't budge through the door. I pushed and pushed but it was like trying to fit a square peg in a round hole. Sphyncus stayed relatively relaxed throughout the whole thing, but she shifted her weight frequently trying to stay on her feet, which only added to the difficulties we were already having.

I stood there balancing my end of the crate against my legs and stomach while the other end rested against the edge of the backseat. It felt like the jumbled up address label was taunting me and I thought about just leaving the crate in the parking lot. Using that frustration as fuel, I lifted it up higher and started pushing as hard as I could while rocking it back and forth. I angled it a little bit, throwing Sphyncus off balance in the process, and the sides finally squeezed in.

We hit the road looking for a place we could stop with an ample amount of grass so Sphyncus could finally get out and stretch her legs. She stood in the crate looking about curiously, no whimpering or whining or barking. It was almost shocking how calm she was. After a few miles, we came upon a gas station with a nice lawn line going down the side.

Randi pulled the car over by a curb and we started the delicate process of getting our Egyptian dog's feet on American soil for the first time. As I pressed the unlocking mechanism on the crate, it hit me that I was about to touch this dog again. This dog that had caused me so much stress and emotional trauma two months prior was about to be in my arms. The last time I had petted Sphyncus she was laying on her back in the dirt a few feet away from Haram Street. Cars were honking and I had just spent an hour trying to convince her to trust me. A few minutes later I would walk away from her and her sad eyes for what I thought would be forever.

Opening the crate door, I quickly clasped the leash to her collar and reached inside. She retreated to the back, tail still whipping up against the inside walls and a big smile on her face. I was concerned that maybe she didn't remember me after all.

I reached once more and she came forward and licked me on the forehead. My heart melted. Either she did remember me or she was just happy to have a friendly person around paying attention to her. It didn't matter. She was happy and with her family, that's what was important. I scratched her head and scooped her up. As soon as her feet touched the concrete, the helicopter tail started up, followed by a whole body shake and her wiggle worm swivel move. I've never seen a dog smile like that before—pure happiness. There wasn't a hint of that in Cairo. It was incredible to see.

We started making our way towards the grass and I noticed her acting funny. Her back slightly arched up and she bent her body to the right. The back-right leg raised off the ground, almost like it locked up which caused her to hobble a little bit. After a few seconds, whatever it was worked itself out. This was different than the hobble she had had in Cairo. That was mostly front leg and this looked more back leg. A strange thing we would have to get checked out. It didn't seem to bother her, more of an inconvenience while in motion but there didn't appear to be any pain.

The concept of the leash didn't seem completely foreign to her. She didn't walk right next to me, but she seemed to understand what it was for and didn't fight. I had to lead her where I wanted her to go, but she didn't tug and wasn't afraid.

Sphyncus stepped up onto the grass like an astronaut setting foot on a new planet; the terrain was totally new and unfamiliar. No matter, she peed almost instantly. I sat down on the grass with her and she didn't know what to do. Part of her looked like she wanted to just get loved on but another part wanted to keep moving since she'd been cooped up so long. After following her around for a few seconds, she flopped over on her back and stretched out with her head between my legs. Her tail swept across the grass over and over like a broom and she flashed her big alligator mouth smile while I scratched her belly. I can't even imagine being a dog that has only known cement and dirt, then experiencing grass for the first time. She was just so happy.

Eventually she got up to move about and sniff some more. I still had my hands on her when she rolled over and I felt something on my finger. Upon closer inspection, it appeared to be a little bit of poop. Eh. Nothing could ruin the moment, not even dog poop on my hand. The poor girl had been in that crate so long we knew she had messed in there. I wiped the poop on the grass and continued following her around. You know you're having the time of your life when you can just brush poop from your finger and move on.

A few minutes later, she pooped and we saw some worms in it. I know worms are a pretty quick fix with medication but it would mean I couldn't take Sphyncus to E-Style and Chewie right away. I was a little disappointed as I wanted to get my three amigos together to get them used to each other.

After a few more minutes exploring the new landscape, Sphyncus looked to be rooting around for something to eat. It was time for her first American meal. With her ribs easily visible, it was going to take some time and work to fatten her up, but this was the beginning of taking on that challenge.

That dog probably would have eaten anything we put in front of her. She thoroughly massacred that can of food. Then, with food all over her nose, she picked up the lid of the can off the ground and tried to run off with it. It was hilarious and a sign of things to come with her scavenging nature, but we had to get that lid out of her mouth before she hurt herself.

I was a little apprehensive to take something out of her mouth. Despite how sweet she was, I kept reminding myself that she was still a street dog that we had only just started interacting with. My fears turned out to be completely unfounded and she let us take it right from her without the slightest hint of the aggression you might expect from a wild dog protecting its meal.

The banging of nearby construction startled her. I had learned about police in Egypt poisoning and shooting baladis right out in the open as horribly inhumane methods of controlling the stray animal population. Any sort of loud booming noise was probably an immediate alarm for the dogs that managed to survive the government-sanctioned killing sprees. The construction clanging had Sphyncus' full and undivided attention. She didn't start panicking at the sound, but she was clearly uncomfortable with it. None of my previous pets had ever been afraid of storms or fireworks, but something was telling me Sphyncus wasn't going to be anything like my previous pets.

We let her stay out in the open grass a little while longer before we started making our way home. Since Sphyncus hadn't been any trouble with anything we needed her to do, I wasn't too worried about trying to get her back into the crate. I scooped her up into my arms, set her front legs inside the door, and nudged her butt forward. Once inside the crate, she spun in a circle a couple of times then made a pitiful grunt as she laid down. We got back in the car and started the drive home to our new life together.

## Chapter 13

Sphyncus slept almost the entire ride back. Occasionally, she would poke her head up to look around through the openings in the crate then lay back down. She was on top of my old Spider-man blanket and surrounded by stuffed animals she had no interest in, quite a difference from sleeping under the back of a car on the hot pavement. The sight of it touched me. The first time I saw this dog asleep I had hoped that she was dead so she wouldn't have to endure another day of pain and torment lurking around every corner. Now she was resting peacefully on a Spider-man blanket.

It was around 4 P.M. when we pulled up to our apartment. First order of business was a walk around the neighborhood to fully test her skills on a leash and let her stretch out some more, but all she wanted to do was stand nearby and smile at us. It hadn't taken long for her to claim us and she was thrilled by it.

I confess I had never adopted a dog from a shelter before. My dog Prissy, that I grew up with, was a sweet black cocker spaniel my parents brought home one night when I was 5 years old. E-Style was a purebred who was intended to be a show dog by her breeders. I'm somewhat embarrassed to admit that now with the person I've become, but I was 19 and in love with Chinese Cresteds; it was the only way I had found to get one. Being my parents' dog, Chewie was brought home by them, I wasn't there for the adoption. Sphyncus was my first experience bringing home a stray or shelter dog.

You can look at pictures on the internet all day of shelter dogs coming home for the first time with their huge smiles, as if they understand they will only know comfort from that day forward, but seeing it in person is such a different thing to behold. Anyone that has brought a dog home like that will know the exact indescribable feeling that I can't find words for. You saved their life and they know it. They know they have you to thank for it and they will do everything possible to make you happy about your decision for the rest of their life. But first, they must smile at you and take it all in. The freedom, the outside air, the love. I don't know how but they know they're going home, even without having ever seen it before. Standing on the sidewalk holding Sphyncus's leash, I don't know which one of us was happier.

Some kids came out of an apartment a few doors down and she growled at them. It was guttural and deep. A mohawk of hair came up from the back of her neck all the way down to her tail. I had never seen that on a dog before. A dog with her mohawk standing next to her dad with his, what a pair we were. She hadn't displayed any sort of aggression over anything before that. She had barely made a sound the entire time.

Being young kids, I would guess around 5 or 6 at the oldest, they weren't too bothered by it. "Oooh!" and then they just ran the other way, doing kid stuff. I should have known right from the start, but it took me a second to put it together that most likely the only kids Sphyncus had ever known were abusive to her.

It made me wonder where that defensive, protective nature was when she was in Cairo. Would growling have scared the kids off and saved her the torment, or would it have drawn the attention of the police and got her shot? The timid, limping dog of Egypt had already transformed into a confident protector in less than a day. The bizarre part was she hadn't yet gone inside the apartment to get territorial about it. Maybe she thought she was protecting me as I had protected her.

We stayed outside a little longer and she was content to just be there soaking up the Kentucky humidity. She was briefly fascinated by a bird and it made me curious if she had ever seen one before. If she had lived her entire life in the vicinity of the HUSA Pyramids before being picked up by ESMA, then she probably hadn't seen many other animals besides baladi dogs and cats. Regardless, she was captivated by that bird and I thought it was wonderful.

The apartment door opened and Randi poked her head out, raising her eyebrows and gritting her teeth as if to say "it's time." I slowly led the way inside.

I don't think Sphyncus had ever had a bath before but for some reason she started shaking as soon as we shut her in the bathroom with us. How did she know what a bathroom was and why was she scared of it? We had dog shampoo, a little pitcher to pour the water, and several old wash cloths. We were anticipating the first bath to be a real pain in the ass, but were completely unprepared for what came next.

Most dogs fight a little bit when you pick them up and put them in the tub but eventually they just give up and take it. They'll look mad or irritated and there may be a few times they try to scramble out again, but generally getting them in the tub is the hardest part. Not with Sphyncus. She cried and fought as if her life depended on it. She clawed, jumped, howled, panted, panicked, climbed—pick any other verb you like. It was completely awful and she never stopped. Water was splashing everywhere and we were soaked. It was a massive struggle to keep her in the tub and I was scratched all over my body from her toenails. They had obviously never been trimmed so it was like swords raking down my torso and legs.

Randi found a little clump between Sphyncus's neck and chest and really went to work on cleaning it. We had been getting dirt and scabs and poop and who knows what else off her so it seemed logical to think this little clump was something of that variety. Well, I don't know what it was, but Sphyncus acted as if we were killing her. Absolute madness. Sphyncus never once bit, growled, or did anything at all resembling aggression, just made the most extreme evasive maneuvers coupled with constant wailing, yelping, and crying. An Egyptian drama queen.

I have no idea how she never got past us to spread her mayhem around the rest of the bathroom. One could only imagine the shitshow of wet toilet paper, candles, hair products, and whatever else flying around like some sort of poltergeist manifesting. I doubted we would be so lucky next time. It was traumatic for all three of us and it had me concerned about how she might act towards us afterward.

I held her in the tub as Randi grabbed a towel and started drying her off. Miraculously, she liked that part. Being rubbed by a soft towel had a soothing effect on her. She was still panting and looking around like she thought doom was impending, but at least the fighting had stopped. She just sat there and shook while being patted down. I grabbed a brush and started going through her hair. She jumped back at first, but it only took a few strokes before she came to enjoy it.

Sphyncus cleaned up really nice. Her filthy brown color had turned into a light, sandy blonde. Sure, the one ear didn't stand up and her ribs were uncomfortably visible, not to mention the various hairless spots on her legs, but she looked beautiful. A totally new dog. Out of everything I thought about throughout the entire two months between first seeing her and giving her that bath, it never once crossed my mind how she would look all cleaned up. Whenever I thought of Sphyncus I thought of something pitiful and dirty, not something proud and majestic.

The apartment had a second bedroom that was mostly filled with my stuff and we had decided that it would be Sphyncus's temporary quarantine. There was a recliner in the middle of the room that we thought she might like to sleep in and plenty of floor space for her toys.

Sphync was sniffing around, checking out everything. There were toys galore but she hadn't shown any interest in them at all. It was sort of sad, like a kid who was robbed of their childhood. She was of that age where toys should be all that mattered but she just looked at them on the floor and didn't know what they were for. I left her in there alone for a second, partly to test her and see what I would come back to, and partly because Randi was making popcorn in the kitchen.

When I came back she launched right into her wiggle worm motion.

It's hard to accurately describe the Sphyncus wiggle worm. Her body appears to be divided into three separate parts--the head, torso, and hips. They are connected by invisible hinges that allow her to have a slithering, snakelike movement while still standing on her legs, slowly creeping forward. It's always accompanied by the tail that goes from helicopter twirls to whipping side to side then back to helicopter twirls. If there is a cuter display of happiness by any creature on this earth, I haven't seen it.

## Chapter 14

Had it not been for all the stress and driving taking a toll, I'm not sure how I would have managed to sleep that first night. My alarm was set thirty minutes earlier than usual and I hoped that would be enough to get Sphyncus taken care of before work. I could already hear her making noises before I got the door open to her room. When I opened it and turned the light on she barked at me then immediately went into her wiggle worm dance. We hung out for a few minutes then I left her to go shower.

When I turned the handle to go in her room again I noticed the door going across the carpet felt sort of strange. Just as I looked down to see what was under it the smell hit me. Sphyncus had pooped directly behind the door and I had smeared it all over the floor. I couldn't even be mad. Maybe 6 months later I would get onto her about it if it happened again, but not then. She was wiggle-worming the whole time I cleaned it up so I had to laugh. Her sweet personality and clown behavior was going to make it extremely hard to get upset with her about things so trivial.

I leashed her up and headed outside to explore the neighborhood in a manner I never had before. Despite living there almost two years, I had never walked the grassy areas behind the nearby apartments until that morning. The dew on the grass wasn't something I had thought about in a long time until I had to walk a dog through it at 4 A.M. Apparently, all the grass spots in the neighborhood were actually minefields of dog poop, but I had never walked through them before to notice.

For almost two years, the neighborhood wasn't much more than a blur through my car windows on the way to work. Walking Sphyncus down the sidewalk before the sun came up I noticed that, despite the total absence of other human beings, the neighborhood felt alive and inviting. Rabbits were out and Sphyncus tugged at her leash wanting to chase them. Stray cats scattered around the dumpsters. Birds tweeted, crickets chirped, spiders built webs in the trees overhanging the sidewalks, just waiting to ruin my day. It was suddenly a whole new world outside my door.

After work we took Sphyncus in for her first vet visit. I told the story for what felt like the hundredth time and the vet, Dr. Paxton, just stared at Sphyncus in amazement. ESMA had put her birth date as January 1, 2010, which would have put her around six and a half months old. Dr. Paxton estimated she could be a little older but probably still under a year. She weighed in at 21 pounds.

The examination continued and he felt the bump on her leg where the fracture had been. I rubbed it as well but Sphyncus didn't react. It seemed to be totally healed. Her teeth were in rough shape, though, and it was recommended we set up a cleaning as soon as possible. There was at least one that would most likely need to be pulled.

Afterward we went outside to do a short interview for the TV station, sort of a follow up to the story when I was still fundraising. When it ran there wasn't nearly the same type of backlash from the viewers as the first time. Maybe it's because I had the dog and wasn't asking the public for financial help, or maybe people just liked a happy ending. Either way, she had become a small time local celebrity among certain circles and we spent a lot of time that first week meeting with various people that had supported us.

The real moment of truth came toward the end of the week, on the day before Chewie's 5th birthday. Sphyncus's worms hadn't shown themselves all day so I decided it was time for her to meet the Hogs. My dynamic duo was about to become a power trio. The Three Amigos, Three Dog Night, the Three Musketeers. Take your pick.

It was important to me that Sphyncus got to know them early just in case she developed any kind of possessiveness over me. I wasn't sure how my heart would take it if they didn't get along. Plus, she needed friends. We still weren't allowing her free range inside the apartment so her relationship with the cats was restricted to just in passing while going outside for walks. They looked horrified and disgusted; Sphyncus looked curious and anxious. I recalled the pictures Mona had sent of her rolling around on her back while surrounded by other dogs, grinning ear to ear. She needed E and Chew to be playmates.

Mom's house had a chain-link fence around the backyard so I took Sphync back there and turned her loose. I expected her to run wild but she just stood around sniffing at things, staying close to me. E and Chew saw us out the window and went absolutely ape-shit. E-Style's little hairless gray body combined with

Chewie's fuzzy white scruff made a maniacal yin yang of barking and insanity. They were dancing on their hind legs and frenetically pawing at the glass.

I opened the door and let E-Style out alone first. "Hey, Horse!" I crouched down to greet her. Being a mostly hairless Chinese Crested, she resembled a little pony so Horse was one of her main nicknames. She came prancing down the back steps, spinning in circles, and hopping around. She no longer cared about Sphyncus, only me.

Sphync came running over to sniff her. E stood still with her tail swaying ever so slightly while Sphyncus continued to nose her entire body. Once Sphync got close to her face, E was done. Her top lip came up revealing her little vampire bat teeth and she let out her throaty warning growl before snapping. Sphyncus jumped back and started swatting at E's face with her right arm in a playful manner.

They both looked at me with their tails wagging, then E turned and went on the sniffing offensive. Sphyncus nervously wagged her tail and gave her the side eye, raising her arm out of insecurity. After a few seconds, E lost interest and laid down on the concrete to soak up the sun. New dog or not, she wasn't about to lose the opportunity to sunbathe.

Chewie had been at the door barking his head off the whole time, so I let him out next. Sphyncus was all over him right from the start. She could sense he wasn't comfortable so she asserted herself at the first opportunity. Chewie has never cared for other dogs; he's only ever loved E and he made sure Sphyncus got the message. The poor little guy kept trying to run away, but

Sphyncus stayed in pursuit. She really needed to sniff him and wouldn't take no for an answer.

He ran from the steps, to the swing, to the house and back to the steps, stopping every so often to snarl. Sphyncus just kept smiling the whole time, like she was just thrilled to be around other dogs. Not only did she not understand that Chewie wasn't interested in her, it's like she didn't even see it. Totally clueless. There was an innocent naiveté to her that made me sort of sad. Even though she had spent the past two months at ESMA surrounded by other dogs, it was painfully obvious that she had no social skills. Those first however many months of her life had been spent just fighting to survive. Much like her confusion with toys, socializing was a part of her life that she was robbed of in Cairo.

Nevertheless, she was making up for it now. After Chew took refuge by the back door, Sphync started running laps around the back yard. It reminded me of the videos you see online where factory farm cows or pigs are rescued and they are let out to frolic freely for the first time in their lives. They start out slowly then spring into life, jumping and running around like baby mice just opening their eyes. That was Sphyncus in my mom's backyard.

Sphyncus turned her attention to E, who had started rolling around in the grass. Sphync sniffed at her belly, resulting in E snapping at her again. I lazily got onto E about it but I couldn't really be upset with her. That had been her yard to dominate up until 5 minutes ago. She had been missing her right eye for a little over a year prior to this, so anybody or anything that came at her from that side was highly likely to startle her and get snapped at. Sphyncus, being oblivious to warning signs, got snapped at repeatedly that first afternoon.

Eventually, mom got home and rushed out back to meet her new "granddogger." Sphyncus took an immediate liking to her and that boded well for the future. Not only would we be spending a lot of time at Mom's place to be with the Hogs, but we'd also be relying on Mom as a babysitter from time to time. She made a comment about what Sphyncus's eyes must have seen and it would be something she'd bring back up every now and then when Sphync had that sad glimmer in them. It was a reminder of what we had done and how far Sphyncus had come. We took the dog out of Cairo but we couldn't take Cairo out of the dog. Those sweet, sad eyes.

The next day, Sphyncus went to work with me. I can't say enough about this dog's bizarre behavior and how it didn't take any time at all to see it. The hallways at the TV station are linoleum but Sphyncus reacted as if they were sheets of ice. Somehow, she just couldn't get her feet under her. She looked like Bambi trying to stand up for the first time.

She pressed her side up against the wall and rubbed up against it the entire way down the hall. It made absolutely no sense and it was hilarious. At the end of the first hallway, she stopped before rounding the corner and had a sort of panicked look on her face. Mouth open, tongue hanging out, eyes wide. In time, it would be classic Sphyncus.

She looked at me and started to turn around. She walked backwards around the corner before spinning to face me and hug against the wall again. Little did I know at the time, but that wouldn't be a one-off approach to rounding corners on a slick surface. This was to be her method permanently.

We went upstairs to the control room where my coworkers were. As soon as we entered the room, Sphyncus saw a mat on the floor and scrambled over to stand on it. After a few minutes of introducing her to people, I took her down to the studio. Being the weirdo that she is, Sphyncus ran from one set to the next, staying off the linoleum as much as possible. The news desk was on a carpeted platform, a place she could stand without flailing around. The interview set was another platform with carpeting, no sliding to be done there. I had no explanation to offer up other than 'she's a street dog, she's probably never been on slick floor like this. I don't know, she's crazy. Isn't she awesome?'

We went back upstairs and she seemed to take a special liking to my friend Ken. He was snacking on animal crackers and pulled one out of the bag to give her. It was a camel.

The words, "Are you happy? Make me happy" repeated in my head. He gave her the camel to eat and she was happy.

Together, we took Sphyncus outside to the field with the satellites and let her run around in the grass. There was something surreal about watching the former street dog go nuts in the grass surrounded by satellites.

After work, we went back to Mom's for Chewie's birthday. I've never personally been a fan of giving dogs things like cake, but Mom treats them like they're actual kids, complete with little birthday parties and candles on cakes that I blow out while holding them up.

Mom placed the little paper plates with cake on them down on the floor in front of each dog. Sphyncus gobbled it up like her life depended on it. She then turned her attention to Chewie's and a fight almost broke out. It's like she knew Chewie wasn't dominant by their interactions the previous day so she preyed on him.

That was the end of the birthday cake for that year. Chewie assumed his little gargoyle perch on the back of the couch and looked pitiful, just like a little kid whose birthday party had been ruined. Sphyncus was clearly the aggressor, but I didn't feel right disciplining her over it. It was her fifth day in America and probably her first time eating cake. How was she supposed to react? Getting Sphyncus acclimated to life as a normal dog was going to be a serious undertaking.

## Chapter 15

There are telltale signs when a dog has done something wrong and gets busted. Head down, tail tucked, sitting in a corner with their teeth showing. Some dogs are proud of their mischief. You've seen the pictures of a living room that looks like a tornado went through it with a dog sitting happily in the middle, clearly waiting for its owner to come home.

Sphyncus does none of those things. She simply moves on with her life and acts oblivious. Whatever it was has already happened and is now in the past. She's got lost time to make up for. Maybe it's some type of street smarts she's employing to seem innocent, as if saying, "I didn't even notice that over there. Is it important? I can't even imagine how it ended up like that. Let's go have fun now." She then gives you a playful look and subtle tail wag.

At this time, Sphyncus was still being kept mostly separate from the cats due to Randi's paranoia about how they might interact when we weren't monitoring, so most of the time indoors was spent in that second bedroom. It became her little hut. Once she became interested in toys, they were all she cared about and they covered the room. If something was on the floor, it was a toy to her.

One night early on, we were sitting in Sphyncus's room playing with her and her toys. We got distracted talking for a few minutes then Randi noticed she couldn't find her phone anywhere. Sphync looked up sheepishly from behind the recliner as her tail started to brush the carpet slowly. That was her sign. She wasn't chewing on the phone or playing with it, just possessing it. It had touched the floor therefore she claimed it. It was as simple as that.

Not long after that, Randi called me, fuming, while I was at work. Between when I went to work and when she had gotten up, Sphyncus had started ripping up the carpet behind the door of her room. She either didn't like being closed in or had severe separation anxiety. Randi's solution was to put her in the crate she flew over in while she went to work. I was adamantly against it but powerless to prevent it. Our first blow up over our new dog.

A few hours later, she called me back in a panic. She'd come home on lunchbreak and found Sphyncus freaking out in the crate. There was a broken tooth on the floor surrounded by blood. I had been afraid something like that would happen. She felt terrible about it but I was still furious.

One of her canine teeth had broken nearly in half. Her teeth were already in bad shape and now this. We had been assured by Dr. Paxton that there was dental work in her future and that future had arrived. Sphyncus has had extensive dental work done since then. A couple more pulled and a lot of cleanings. I still have that piece of broken tooth in a box.

Sphyncus never stepped in that crate again. For the time being, we kept shutting her in the bedroom while we were at work and just accepted that she would continue 'renovating' it for us. The damage had already been done. The deposit on the place was as good as gone.

This may make me sound like an asshole but I saw a little bit of poetic justice in the whole thing. Randi was the one not comfortable leaving her out around the cats while we were gone. We had seen nothing to suggest problems, but she wouldn't relent. If you take a street dog and shut her up in a room over and over again she was bound to get destructive.

At some point, we employed the strategy of pulling her crate up against the back of the door when closing it. It was a futile attempt to prevent her from having direct access to her target. Her first reaction was to start going to work on the window sill before she figured out she could butt up against the crate and move it away. She wanted out of that room badly and the sooner we trusted her, the better.

Of course, Randi's argument was "if she's doing it to that room we don't want her doing it to the whole apartment. The lease is in my name and I don't want to risk it."

I pointed out that I hadn't rescued this dog from the streets just to shut her in a room five days a week while we were at work. She responded by telling me how much Sphyncus liked to chase the cats when given the chance and she didn't want that going on all day. I reminded her how the cats constantly got on the counters and there was even a basket for them on top of the refrigerator under a vent that only encouraged it. More words were exchanged and nothing was solved.

This was the beginning of Randi's resentment towards me for bringing Sphyncus into her and the cats' lives without even discussing it. She loved Sphyncus but, like I said before, I never consulted her about it. I just did it and she had to deal with it. This was a risk I took and I knew it all along. I did it because I had to; consequences be damned. I was now learning of the consequences and, unfortunately for Sphyncus, she had to take the brunt of it.

The more I pressed the issue, the more the bickering turned into arguing. She became less lenient with Sphyncus and came down even harder on me each time more damage was done. I retaliated by being more vocal when getting onto the cats for everything they weren't supposed to be allowed to do but continuously got away with. It's petty and I loved the cats, but it was the only weapon I had in my arsenal to fight back with.

Since the only thing "wrong" the cats ever really did was get on the counter, I had to find additional things to even the score. It was only fair that if Sphyncus wasn't allowed full range of the apartment then I wasn't going to allow the cats into her room. They loved going in there to try to steal her food or find new hiding places so I started getting onto them for it every chance I got. I'd blast out "Bengal!" or "Chewy!" in a really short, powerful burst and they would be off to the races, skidding down the hallway or diving off the countertop.

The icing on the cake is I inadvertently taught Sphyncus their names by doing it. She was so desperate to not be in trouble all the time that she couldn't wait to see the cats being scolded. She would come flying into the room and sliding across the floor, stopping within inches of whichever cat it was. They were frozen solid and Sphyncus would stare down at them. I was like the bully in the high school movies and she was the guy standing behind me always running running his mouth.

If it were Karate Kid, I was Johnny and she was on the sidelines yelling, "Get 'em a body bag!"

I felt bad for the cats. It wasn't their fault and I was using them as pawns in my battle with their mom, but after a while it became sort of hilarious. Even Randi eventually found it funny just because of how consistent Sphyncus was about it and how quickly she could go from dead asleep in her recliner to staring down a cat in the living room. Zero to a hundred in the span of a cat's name. We started referring to her as Sheriff Sphyncus because she had to maintain the law.

I knew the time would finally come when enough was enough. Every day the room was more torn up than the day before. The scratches on the wall turned into a huge spot in the paint disappearing entirely, revealing the drywall behind it. Shortly after, there was a small hole. The back of the door developed a hole of its own, big enough to fit a basketball inside. Fortunately, she never actually tore all the way through to the other side. The carpet had a spot the size of a doormat completely ripped away. It became a mangled mess of strings and matting on the floor, so we had to cut it off in a clean line just to be able to shut the door. You'd think that would be enough to put a stop to shutting her in there, but no. The worst was yet to come.

One afternoon when I got off work, my stomach was in knots. I let Sphyncus out of her prison and headed straight into the bathroom. Being the only person home, I left the door open. As I'm sitting on the toilet, I see Sphync running back and forth in the hallway pawing at her face. She was in a full-blown hysteria, galloping around with her mouth open continuously digging at it. All I could do was sit there and watch until things calmed down on my end. Initially, I was worried she might be choking so I debated leaving the toilet to check on her, making the most disgusting mess of all time in the process if I had to. When I didn't hear her gasping for air, I knew it wasn't life threatening so I waited it out.

Finally in the clear, I rushed over to see what was going on. There was a piece of wood stuck in her mouth and it was wedged between the top two front teeth. It was obviously wood from the door frame in her room where she'd be tearing it up all day, but I had no idea how long it had been stuck in her mouth or how badly it was lodged. There wasn't any blood but I feared it might be stuck in the palate of her mouth since she couldn't get it out.

Aside from the bath incident, Sphyncus had been nothing but loving and cooperative since we got her. Nevertheless, I was always still very apprehensive in those early days when doing anything that was invasive with her, such as pulling a piece of wood out of her mouth. You never know how a terrified dog is going to react.

I took a deep breath and pulled the wood straight down. It slid from top to bottom like a thick piece of floss. Sphyncus's temperament immediately changed. She licked me on the hand and wiggle wormed over to her water bowl.

That evening I told Randi the story and she finally agreed. It was time to show Sphyncus the trust she had shown us.

## Chapter 16

If you could sum up Sphyncus's behavior in one word it would be "why?" Not long after giving her free rein of the apartment, I started coming home to find one of her toys randomly standing up in places. The key to this is that it's not a stuffed animal or something bottom-heavy that might balance on its own; it's a rubber squeaky-toy donkey piñata that has legs. It's about the size and shape of a toy horse that an action figure would ride on and it must be placed standing on its legs to do that. I almost never saw it just laying around on its side the way it would if you dropped it. It became a game after the first couple of times I found it. I'd open the apartment door to see it standing there waiting like a butler and Sphyncus would come wiggle worming around the corner like there was nothing unusual about it. I'd find it standing in the living room watching over the other toys, sometimes it would be standing in her bedroom.

One time in particular has always stood out. I got up in the middle of the night to go to the bathroom and when I turned on the light I saw something in my peripheral vision. The piñata was standing guard, like some sort of night sentry posted in the hallway. It was a little creepy being half awake and turning around to find I was being stared at by a lifeless, rainbow colored mystery donkey.

I don't think I've ever been so interested in something in my life. I had to know how she was doing it, but I had no idea how to catch her in the act without an elaborate camera set up. In my mind, it was something she was intentionally doing for whatever reason her baladi brain came up with, like she would set it down and it would fall over so she'd pick it back up and try again until it was right. I had to know.

One evening we came home and Sphyncus was extra excited—running around, grabbing toys and scattering them everywhere. Of course, the piñata was already standing up in her bedroom so she grabbed it and ran around the corner towards the front door. My eyes were glued to her. She gently lowered her head and set it down in the exact opposite motion of how she picked it up. She treated it as if it was breakable and the toy would shatter if she dropped it. It was a very delicate procedure, one I've never seen another dog do.

Was there something significant about the piñata and the way it fit in her mouth that made her put it down in such a way? Was it something she did for us like a cat bringing you its kill? Was it for pride? Because she's weird? The world may never know.

In addition to all of her own toys that we bought for her, Sphyncus also had the majority of E-Style and Chewie's old toys that they no longer played with. Stuffed animals, nylabones, squeakies, you name it. They had to be as spread out as possible across the apartment in some sort of bizarre territorial marking. Every room needed toys in case she had the urge to play or chew at any second, which she commonly did totally out of the blue. Once she finally saw their value, they were the only things that mattered.

The toy obsession went further than just inside the walls of the apartment. For a long time, whenever I would grab her leash, she would respond by grabbing a toy to take with us. It was usually a stuffed animal of some kind, most likely with a squeaker. We'd hit the sidewalks in the neighborhood as if walking the runway at a fashion show--Sphyncus proudly carrying her flavor-of-the-week plaything and me proudly walking my Sphyncus.

Occasionally, she'd drop it on the ground to sniff out the messages left by the dogs before her. When she was satisfied that all the intelligence had been properly gathered, she'd be on her merry little way but she would never pick the toy back up. I couldn't just leave her friends behind for some other dog to claim so then I would be stuck walking around with a yellow stuffed bear or squeaky hotdog in hand. Let me tell you, you get a lot of smiles from your neighbors when you're walking around holding a rubber hotdog.

The funniest part of the toys-go-for-walks phase is that eventually she'd turn to look at me and see that I had her toy. She'd suddenly remember how important it was to her and lunge at my hand to get it back. I'd hand it over and we'd repeat the cycle until we got home. Sometimes, if the toy was small enough, I would put it in my back pocket for the remainder of the walk after she dropped it enough times.

One morning when I got up for work, I threw on the same shorts I'd worn the day before and went into the kitchen to sit down with a bowl of cereal. As soon as my butt hit the stool, out came the loudest squeak of all time. Like a whoopie cushion, only instead of a fart sound it was the shrill wheezing of a squeaker. The full weight of my body came down on it in my back pocket and it responded by sounding the alarms. Sphyncus was out of her chair and standing looking up at me within a second. Eyes wide, one ear up, body at full attention, she wanted answers. I got up and reached into my pocket pulling out her little purple rubber pig. She grabbed it from my hand and promptly took it to bed with her.

That little purple pig completely consumed Sphyncus for a little while. Unlike many of her other rubber squeaky toys, she never attempted to get the squeaker out. It would live on forever if she had anything to say about it. She was so fixated on it that she would often have another toy in her mouth then go pick up the rubber pig as well. Sometimes it would be a big rawhide bone sticking out of both sides of her mouth with the purple pig in front like a gate keeper. I liked to imagine the pig was guarding the bone, letting out a deafening screech if you got too close to its prized possession.

The only problem was that Sphyncus couldn't bite down on the pig due to the hard rawhide behind it in her jaws so she would mimic the sound of the squeaker herself. She trotted from room to room with the bone and pig combo in her mouth, imitating the squeak in her throat. She'd stop and look around with her eyes wide and curious, then run to a different room to repeat it. Of all the hilarious, peculiar things she does that has always been one of my favorites.

Much like how E-Style had her little spot known as the Batcave, Sphyncus has Batcaves of her own. Whereas E used hers as a hiding place to hoard bones and toys, Sphyncus's Batcaves are more of a nontraditional means of getting from one place to another. In the old Batman movies and comics there were several different methods used to disguise the outside entrance to the cave: an actual cavern, behind a waterfall, and a hologram among others. Sphyncus will sometimes, entirely at random, choose to crawl under a chair or table rather than go around them. Hence, her Batcaves. Similar to turning around backwards to go around corners on slick floors, I've never been able to find a reason why she does these things. It's inconsistent and purposeless.

We had a short end table beside the loveseat that was the original Sphyncus Batcave. The table had a trestle base and it was situated so that the opening between the legs was perpendicular to the side of the loveseat. The apartment was small so an open spot under a table like that was a great place to put things on the floor and have them still be out of the way.

One day when there wasn't much laying under the table Sphyncus took a detour and dove through the opening underneath instead of the more obvious path of walking around it. As funny as it was, I didn't understand why she did it and that was becoming a recurring theme.

The real test of the Batcave came a few days later when she made for it again but this time it had the usual clutter underneath. She darted towards it, stopped and stepped back looking confused, lunged forward again, hopped back once more, then plowed right through sending shoes, purses, and backpacks flying all over the room. It looked like a bomb of footwear and bags had detonated.

If she had just run straight through it on the first try it would have no doubt been hysterical, but her thought process was the hilarious part. Flat out ridiculous in the best possible way. I think that was the first time I truly knew that Sphyncus is an absolute maniac. She wanted so badly to take this unconventional little passage that she actually stopped, contemplated it twice, then charged forward right through it. She gets a wide-eyed panicked look when faced with something like that, it was the exact same look she had at the TV station when she approached the corners backwards. Anxiety overcomes her and it causes her to then make an irrational decision on how to handle the obstacle, which then becomes a habit for all future instances. I'll say this for her, as unorthodox and ungraceful as her techniques may be, Sphyncus solves whatever problems stand in her way.

One evening, we weren't watching her as closely as we should have been so we didn't pick up on the signs that she needed to go outside to potty. Randi looked down the hall and Sphyncus was squatting down over the cats' litter box.

I'm sure there are dogs out there that have been trained to use litter boxes, but I've personally never known of them. I've certainly never seen a dog learn how to use something by watching cats rather than being trained by a human.

One of the most surprising things about Sphyncus is that she doesn't like the heat. I don't know if it's because she was born into it or what, but once she set foot in the Bluegrass State she turned her back on Ra, the sun god of her ancestors. Without hesitation, she forsook the ancient ways in favor of a new god: air conditioning. This was my little street dog from the

Josh Hines

Middle East, tough as nails! Nagat, the survivor! No, that dog was gone. This was Sphyncus the couch dog. She doesn't bathe in the sun, only in luxury and excess.

E-Style is a sun dog through and through. She loves nothing more than cooking on the pavement and evening out the farmer's tan she develops every winter while wearing clothes. I fully anticipated Sphyncus giving her a run for her money. Alas, the baladi from the desert would much rather lay on the cool laminate floor inside.

Don't get me wrong; this dog loves walks. Long walks, in fact. Just not in the summer. Summer walks consist of standing on the sidewalk aimlessly then crossing the street back and forth repeatedly before she finally makes for the door again.

When fall came around I really learned all about having a young, athletic dog that has enough energy to power the entire city. We walked several miles every day. Sometimes we took as many as four or five walks in a single day. Once before work, again on lunch break, immediately after work, another a few hours later that would be the longest, then another short walk before bed.

She spoiled me the first few months when it was still hot out. I didn't think she would require a lot of exercise, but I was so very wrong. There isn't a blade of grass in my neighborhood that I don't know now. There were buildings, fields, schools, streets, and disc golf courses in my direct vicinity that I had no idea existed before Sphyncus started taking me on daily expeditions. I didn't even know all the different ways out of my neighborhood until she started leading me around. No

128

step left untaken. No bush left un-sniffed. No yard left un-peed on.

It wasn't long before the Egyptian dog got her first taste of snow. November rolled around and we got a light dusting overnight. As soon as the door opened, she stopped dead in her tracks and just stared. After a gentle tug on her leash, she very carefully stepped out into it. She stopped, sniffed, bit at it, then totally lost control. She started leaping, running, thrashing about, and pulling me along behind her. I thought she might put on a show for me, but I underestimated how wild she would get. I can only imagine what a sight that was at 4:15 in the morning—me laughing hysterically at her while she ran amok in the parking lot. Work that day consisted of little more than me being anxious to get back home to play in the snow with my dog. I felt like a kid again.

When my lunch break rolled around, I went home and immediately leashed Sphync back up. Right on cue, she started frolicking all over the place, kicking snow everywhere, and having the time of her life. As much as I hadn't predicted she would shun the summer sun like she had, it was equally unexpected that she would love the winter and snow so much.

She pulled out her savant-like problem solving skills once again and stunned me. Our parking lot sloped downhill then flattened out at the bottom. There were various cracks where the two angles met and one of them had formed a small hole that had an ice sheet going across it. In the midst of her insanity, Sphyncus became intrigued by that little frozen pool. She stared like she was trying to melt it with her eyes then started bashing it with her paw. With busted ice shards scattered about, she leaned down to drink the cold water underneath. I was amazed. How would a dog from Egypt know anything about ice? How would she have any instincts at all for something like that? The Egyptian Eskimo. The Snow Wolf.

That Christmas my brother came into town for the holidays and was staying at our mom's. It was his first trip back home since Sphyncus's arrival and he was excited to meet her. When we walked in she wiggle-wormed across the living room over to Mom while E and Chew barked at her. A typical entrance. She eventually got on the couch with Smitty and, after a short period of uncertainty, warmed up to him.

The next morning she barked at him again for a few minutes before coming to her senses and calming down. She had seemed to really like him the night before, so it came out of nowhere. It was still too early to know it at the time, as she hadn't been around most people more than once or twice, but it would be the manner in which all of her relationships with people were formed. Barking incessantly, then apprehensive for a while, finally looking like she was warming up to them, then acting like they were a complete stranger the next time she saw them.

Numerous encounters later she might finally be happy to see the same person again. Or she might not. Some people have been hated enemies for months then one day at random she decides to love them. It's just another bizarre way of doing things for a dog that has no shortage of bizarre behaviors.

Chapter 17

One month later, the Egyptian Revolution of 2011 began. Also known as the January 25th Revolution, it lasted two and a half weeks and completely shut down Egypt's tourism. To this date it has still never fully recovered.

As a foreigner, I don't feel it's appropriate to comment on the details of why it happened and what it was about, but I do recognize the importance of it. More so, I understand that Cairo was described by many as a war zone and that if Sphyncus had still been on the streets during that time the chances of her survival would have plummeted. All in all, 846 people were said to have died, over 6,000 more were injured, and over 12,000 were arrested. It is unknown and untold how many animals suffered and died.

I don't want to get into the politics of it all, but I do want to touch upon some personal stories I've been told regarding the situation with animals in Egypt during that time.

My own firsthand experiences there 8 months earlier let me see how dependent on tourism a lot of Egyptians are. The scammers that got us at the Pyramids were entirely reliant on it. The focal point of their operation was the two camels they suckered us onto. Without tourism those men would have had no means of providing for themselves, so they would have no more use for the camels. During the revolution the camels were most likely left around the stables to fend for themselves, meaning they would have ultimately starved to death. That's the story of countless camels, donkeys, and horses in the Giza area.

ESMA and other animal rescue groups took in so many animals that they lost count. New cases were coming in all day every day and many of those are still with them all these years later. Foreigners left in droves and either left their animals behind on the streets or turned them over to guards and porters under the assumption they would take care of them. Rioting and looting caused food shortages, resulting in a lot of those animals starving to death.

Once the government curfew came down it made it even harder to get from place to place, which in turn made it more difficult to keep providing for personal pets or animals left in one's care. Pet shops were raided and ransacked, especially those near Tahrir Square. Some of the wealthy citizens had their homes set on fire with dogs and horses still inside and on the property.

Mona Khalil relayed the following to me: "With the riots that were going and the thugs that went down on the night of January 28th and started robbing all shops and supermarkets, attacking villas and apartments... People had to start going down themselves and making guarding groups in every street, improvising in defensive ways.

"The only thing that made us a bit relieved was when the army came down on the street. We started breathing. We trust our army a lot. The economic situation had its immediate toll, of course, and tourism stopped immediately. We had animals dying of lack of food, like in the area where you stayed. This is where we (ESMA) went down to work in February after seeing dead horses and donkeys and camels. Of course, in areas where there were fights and fires, dogs and cats on the street suffered a lot. Especially at the hands of the MB (Muslim Brotherhood) members who look on dogs as dirt. In some areas they used them to set fires in places.

"Yes, surely Sphyncus would not have survived. The area where she used to live has many of the extremist groups and MB members and is one of the difficult areas. Surely we suffered to get to the shelter with the curfew and finding supplies and to find money in the first place to get supplies and for our workers who were torn between keeping the place safe and their homes safe."

I've been told other stories about police officers disappearing from the streets for days, leaving the neighborhoods and compounds to look after themselves. Those that stayed set up checkpoints and used dogs to help secure the area. Everyone involved gained a new appreciation for their dogs as they provided protection and acted as alarms. I don't care who you are or how big the dog is, nobody wants to get bitten by a dog. I don't like the idea of animals being used for security purposes, but we all know it works. An intruder is much less likely to break into a place with a barking dog.

Sadly, if some people were putting animals to work for nobler purposes, it would be expected that others would find more detestable usage for them. A friend of mine told me she saw a woman riding a camel pulling a cart of stolen items. Imagine a camel cart with a big, brand new TV sticking out of it--the most contrasting visual I can think of.

Of course, there are far worse stories like the one Mona mentioned of dogs being used to start and spread fires. Brutality and barbarism at its absolute worst.

Growing up and living my entire life in rural America, I cannot in anyway identify with or relate to any of the things that the Egyptian people went through during the revolution or as a result of it. Watching it happen on the news, I only felt happy that we were able to get Sphyncus out of there when we did, and I felt grief for all of the others like her that didn't make it. I didn't know what else to think. It was hard to imagine the area I stayed in just 8 months earlier being overrun with anarchy.

Even though at that time I still very much looked down on Cairo and the people I had interacted with while there, I still felt incredibly sad about everything going on. Aside from the kids chasing and hitting Sphyncus, I didn't see any other open displays of outright cruelty. I saw extreme carelessness, selfishness, and negligence, but nothing worthy of what the people there must have been dealing with on a daily basis. Like so many other times throughout history, the animals were innocent bystanders that ultimately suffered the most. They deserved better.

Listening to Mona describe the work of ESMA on a normal day is heartbreaking enough, but that time period in particular was agonizing. The helplessness I felt while trying to help one baladi dog was no comparison to how powerless they must have felt watching dozens and dozens starve and languish at every turn. Every time I saw another update of the

rioting in Cairo on the television or the internet I hugged
Sphyncus a little tighter.

Chapter 18

Sphyncus was growing more comfortable in her new life and developing a lot of new behaviors along the way. Some good, some bad. She became very territorial over the apartment and the neighborhood.

It became tiresome to have company over as she would bark the entire time, only backing down in the presence of large groups. She would still walk around huffing and puffing and didn't want anyone petting her, but the noise would die down the more crowded it got. It started taking her longer and longer to trust new people. She has an inner circle of a few close members and that's enough for her. I'm not going to lie, it's both frustrating and annoying.

E and Chew have never taken to new people immediately, but after they're inside for a few minutes they calm down. Typically, they'll both end up in the visitor's lap before the evening is over. Sphyncus is a different story. Her behavior toward new people can be an absolute nightmare to deal with.

She barks at everyone and everything—and sometimes at absolutely nothing. For a dog that was so pitiful and quiet when taking abuse, she quickly became dominant in her second life. She tries to strike fear into every person she meets by raising her hackles and screaming at them. A guttural growl emerges from the depths and her eyes go wild. If the person is nervous, she instantly picks up on it and preys on them. I have friends that Sphyncus scared when they first met her, and she's never forgotten it. Even after settling down, she still picks them out of a crowd and targets them each time. It would almost be funny if it wasn't so irritating. I'm not saying she doesn't have every reason to be skeptical of people, because she certainly does, it's just exhausting dealing with it every single day.

She hates almost every other dog that's not E and Chew. She wants to chase every cat that isn't Bengal and Chewy. If it's another type of animal then she's definitely chasing it. Her obsession with rabbits and squirrels is far beyond normal dog behavior. It's been the source of a few laughs, but she's also gotten in quite a bit of trouble because of it.

I found several places in our neighborhood I felt comfortable letting her off the leash to run around. They were either entirely fenced in or mostly fenced in with buildings or trees on the open sides. One day I let her in the fence surrounding a school after hours. She ran to a spot and stopped, spinning in circles looking completely confused. Rabbits popped up from all around her and took off in every direction.

Sphyncus continued to spin and hop around, but she didn't know which one to chase so she ended up just running laps around the field in an all-out frenzy. A collection of rabbits seemed to be what she always wanted, but she didn't know how to handle them going off every which way. I can't imagine the reasoning behind what she did. "Well, if I can't chase them all then I won't chase any. I guess I'll just run full speed in a circle like a Nascar race until my heart feels like it's going to explode."

One fateful evening, Sphyncus caught one. She started stalking a row of bushes, so I knew something had to be in there but hoped it would have the survival instincts to not come out. If you've never heard a rabbit scream, then consider yourself lucky. It's horrifying.

This tiny little bunny came dashing out of the bushes with Sphyncus in hot pursuit and it let out the most pitiful little screech. It stopped and hunkered down in the grass as if it just gave up and accepted its fate. Sphyncus stood and stared down at it. I ran over and leashed her up. The poor bunny just sat in the grass shaking. I kept the leash tight and reached down to stroke its back expecting it to run again but it stayed. Just trembling. It was the saddest thing.

Even though I wasn't about to let her loose again, I felt Sphyncus earned the right to at least finally see up close what she had been obsessing over for so long. Of all the rabbits she had chased, this one finally got caught. Holding the leash tight, I let Sphync lower her head to sniff it. Her nose was dripping like she was salivating. She gave the bunny a good lick down the back then looked up at me smiling. She was so proud of herself. Surprisingly, when I tugged on her leash to go home she didn't fight me. I expected a battle since we were leaving her prize behind, but it was almost like knowing she finally outran one was enough for her.

Not long after finding herself in the middle of a bunch of rabbits, Sphyncus found herself in a significantly worse predicament. We had discovered a disc golf course close by that was in a wooded area, another place I could unleash her to run around. She heard something rustling in the tall grass, so she leapt in to investigate. I stood outside of it, about 20 or so feet away. After a few seconds, she raised her paw up and stood completely stiff. A series of small white clouds floated up and encircled her. It looked like numerous fluffy puff balls of dandelion seeds rising out of the ground waiting for her to blow them into the air. I was utterly dumbfounded as to what I was seeing. It made absolutely no sense. Until it did.

I yelled her name at the top of my lungs and she sprang up straight in the air like a scared cat. She came bounding out and we both started to run. A couple of seconds is all it took before the smell started wafting toward us. Skunks. She had been standing in the middle of a bunch of skunks. The white puffs were their tails. We didn't just dodge a bullet, we dodged an atomic bomb.

Regrettably, this wouldn't be Sphyncus's only encounter with skunks. Her penchant for chasing rabbits extended to all wildlife so, despite escaping from their circle of doom, she would still chase them one on one every chance she got. Eventually, she got blasted by one and I had to walk her all the way home so the smell wouldn't get in the car. I wasn't mad at her, if anything it was my fault. A dog is going to be a dog. It was me that continued to let her off the leash to act like a maniac, knowing she would chase anything that moves. We both learned our lesson that night.

Oddly enough, the one thing about her that hardly changed at all for a long time was her weight. In the beginning, she ate whatever was in front of her but it didn't take long for her to develop this grazing attitude towards food. She'd get around to eating it whenever she felt like it. Sometimes that meant the food sat out for a while and, in the case of wet food, might need to be thrown out. She was being fed properly for the first time in her life but decided beggars could, in fact, be choosers. It was common to be stared at while taking walks because of how thin she was and I had countless conversations with people about it. It took a good three years before she fully started looking healthy.

At the advice of other baladi owners, we started her out on organic food but at the vet's advice switched to regular food since she either lost her appetite or grew tired of it. We tried every brand of food over the first couple of years. We tried high calorie food, puppy food, wet food, dry food, anything anyone suggested. Out of all the strange things about Sphyncus, her not gaining weight was by far the most unexpected and difficult to solve.

I started to play mind games with her to try to get her to eat better. Using her dry food as treats when learning new tricks, putting different things on the food like broths and cheese to entice her, and taking uneaten food away so she couldn't graze. Frustration got the better of me one evening so I took to playfully taunting her with the food. I took the dry pebbles and drew a big picture of her on the floor standing next to her empty bowl.

I have these stick figure drawings of the Hogs I like to do whenever I get the chance and I even have stickers made of them to put around places, so I drew the stick figure version of Sphyncus out on the floor. She never once interrupted me while doing the drawing and let me completely finish before approaching. Episodes like that started to become known as The Riddle of the Sphyncus.

It's almost customary for dogs to be scared of fireworks and thunderstorms but, like most things in life, Sphyncus takes it to the next level. Luckily for us, the Fourth of July had already passed when Sphync arrived, but we got hit hard with it in the summer of 2011. I don't know how often fireworks are used in celebration in Egypt so maybe she'd never seen or heard them before, but they terrify her. Given the situation in her home country with police shooting strays it's possible, even likely, that Sphyncus had witnessed other dogs being shot. Maybe even her own family. Whatever the case may be, any sort of popping sound sends her into a panic. E-Style and Chewie never reacted to anything the way Sphyncus reacts to fireworks and storms so, once again, we were in uncharted waters on how to handle it.

When I say "panic," I'm not talking about her wide-eyed look that accompanies a tail-tucked trembling or her hiding under the table panting. I'm talking about being woken up in the middle of the night because it feels like an earthquake is throwing the bed around the room but it's actually just Sphyncus violently shaking. I'm talking about her repeatedly ramming into a closed door hard enough to open it. The kind of convulsing that makes me legitimately worry she's going to have a heart attack.

We had moderate success with a Thunder Shirt, but it merely lessened the height of the episode. It didn't prevent it or make it subside. We consulted Dr. Paxton and he prescribed a pill for her called alprazolam that is essentially dog Xanax. A half of one of those, wait about 15 minutes or so, and she's high as a kite. Not a care in the world anymore. A positive side effect is she wants to eat everything in sight so on those days we kill two birds with one stone.

In August of 2011, I made one of the only decisions I've ever regretted with Sphyncus. We boarded her for five days. Randi found a deal online for a trip to Myrtle Beach and we knew Sphyncus wouldn't enjoy the crowds or the atmosphere. We wanted to take her to a beach, but that wasn't the right time or place. My mom wasn't available to act as a sitter, so it was either not go or board Sphyncus to see how she did.

We found a place locally called Dog's Day Out that had by far the best ratings in the area. They have staff on site 24 hours a day, the dogs can stay in runs rather than just kennels, they get one on one attention, and plenty of outside time. It was pricey but sounded excellent. If it all worked out, then it might be an option we would have in the future if the situation called for it.

Our plan was to drive through the night so we had to drop Sphyncus off right before business hours ended at 6 P.M. I don't know how dogs sense the things that they do, but she knew we were leaving her there. Her sad eyes looked downright depressed and lost. She must have thought we were abandoning her. To make matters worse, it started to storm right before we left. It was hard to not just call the whole thing off and take her back home with us, but we had to at least give boarding one try.

To no one's surprise I called to check on her every day. At first, she wasn't eating at all so a staff member took to rolling her dry food up in peanut butter balls. The next day I was told she had been biting at the cage bars of the run. Sadly, she wasn't getting along well with the other dogs so she had to be kept alone and taken outside to a fenced in area by herself.

We got home late Sunday night, so we couldn't pick her up until the next day. The apartment felt so quiet and lonely the few hours we were awake without her. The next morning, I went out on my lunchbreak to pick her up. Due to my early schedule, I get an hour long break any time between 8 and 10 A.M., so thankfully Sphyncus could come home without having to spend most of another day out there.

When they brought her out she acted as if she didn't even want to see me. My heart broke a little bit. She indeed thought she had been abandoned. The entire ride home she acted indifferent to everything. No interest when I spoke to her, no interest in looking out the window. She was like a zombie. That evening she still seemed apathetic about anything I tried to get her to do. The little shit was holding a grudge and making me feel even worse than I already felt. Thankfully, the next day she woke up in her own home, in her recliner in her room, surrounded by her toys, and seemed to forget all about it. I vowed to never board her again.

A month later, Sphyncus and Randi got their first real test together. I was going on a two-week long road trip out west with my brother Smitty, cousin David, and friend Matt. It was to be the "Great American Road Trip" where we took Route 66 out to California and came back home via the northern route. Randi had decided to stay in town so that meant she would watch Sphyncus while I was gone. I was hoping that would mean they would finally bond. Don't get me wrong; Sphyncus adored Randi and Randi loved Sphyncus, but they weren't bonded in the same way that Sphyncus and I were. Remnants of the resentment towards me and how much Sphyncus had changed our lives were still lingering over a year after adopting her. Something needed to change. The road trip wasn't about forcing the two of them to be stuck together for a couple of weeks, but I recognized that it was a byproduct of it and hoped their time together would bring them closer. I've always traveled as often as I can afford it so this was a good test run to see how Sphyncus would handle something longer than a weekend.

I checked in every day and was pleased with how it sounded like everything was going. The walks weren't as adventurous or as long or as numerous as usual, but it all went smoothly. Randi attempted to make Sphyncus jog with her but that only lasted two days because Sphync hated it. At the end of the two weeks, we rolled back into town around 1 A.M. and I was greeted at the door by Sphyncus holding a squeaky hamburger in her mouth. They were both happy to see me, but Sphync was beside herself. It was a nonstop wiggle worm party for the rest of the night. She brought me all her toys and spun in circles. She barked and growled at me, leapt on and off the furniture. Her little dog brain must have thought I was never coming back.

A year later, we finally got to take Sphyncus to the beach. My family rented a condo for a week in Gulf Shores, Alabama. It's not a truly private beach but there are no hotels around, just other condos. That meant that there were no large crowds, so well-behaved dogs could run freely off leash. I was ecstatic. E-Style was 11 years old by then and I had never taken her to the beach before. It was a lifelong goal but, for whatever reason, something always got in the way.

As much as everyone associates Egypt with sand, a place like Cairo really doesn't have any. If you get out into the desert around the Pyramids, you'll find sand, but it has a dirt quality to it. The Gulf Shores sand experience was like the first time Sphyncus stepped onto the grass at the gas station in Atlanta--she was an interstellar explorer walking out onto the surface of a newly discovered celestial body. A total unknown. Just like she had with the snow, as soon as I unclipped the leash from her collar she began thrashing around and flinging it everywhere. Running laps, kicking up particles into a cloud that followed her every paw print. The Sand Shark was born.

Our second to last day at the beach delivered to me what people refer to as "your happy place." Three days after coming home from Gulf Shores, David and I would be going to South America for two weeks. I'd spent the entire time at the beach trying to really take it all in with the Hogs since I'd be leaving so soon.

The condo was high enough on stilts that you could walk under it, so I took some towels down underneath and sat on the sand. It was late afternoon in September, the heat wasn't bad by that point and we were out of the direct sun. There was a cool breeze coming in off the ocean. Nobody else was out as far as I could see. Only the sound of the waves coming in. The Hogs laid down on another towel nearby and I pulled out a book. Soon I found myself unable to read without distraction. Not the typical distraction of noise or disturbances--I was distracted by how perfect everything was. I couldn't focus on anything else. For once in my life, I was able to just sit and absorb all that was around me.

It was peace.

For just a couple of short hours, I experienced heaven on Earth. It was one of those times that once it's gone, it's gone. You have to appreciate it and soak it all up because you might never attain serenity on the same level ever again. It's lived in my head for years and I'll always long to live it again. Nothing else has compared to it and I fear nothing else ever will. I'll never stop chasing that feeling, my happy place on the beach with The Hogs.

## Chapter 19

A year later, in the fall of 2013, a unique opportunity presented itself. After my stepdad Mark and mom divorced in 2008, he bought a house that he shared with his brother for a short time. It sits on a corner and the previous occupants made substantial add-ons that made it ideal for roommates. Each side of the house has its own driveway, garage, and living room. It has an upstairs master bedroom and two more bedrooms downstairs. Basically, whoever lived there shares the kitchen but has their own everything else.

Mark was looking to sell or rent it, so my mom approached him about renting it to her, Randi, and me. A couple years earlier Mom had moved out of the house with the fenced in yard and into a very small apartment in a fairly rough neighborhood. I wasn't crazy about the idea of living with my mom again at the age of 32, but I did see potential in the arrangement. I would live with all three of the Hogs for the first time. E-Style was 12 years old by then, so I'd be able to live out her last years with her.

There was a small backyard with a privacy fence; it would be much easier to have somebody watch the animals if work went late or when vacations came up. I'd have a garage my bands could practice in. It was much bigger than our apartment and we wouldn't be paying much more. Mom would be in a better place for however long we all lived there. The best part was it was just a couple of streets over from our apartment. Sphyncus would still have her old stomping grounds.

The main cause for alarm was putting the three of us in the same house. Mom and Randi never got along great and, honestly, Mom and I don't get along that well sometimes, either. After a lot of debate, weighing out the pros and cons and drawing up ground rules, we came to an agreement. On October 1st, 2013 we moved into the house. Randi and I took the upstairs bedroom and mom took the two downstairs.

Having more space to maneuver, a staircase to fly up and down, and a backyard to roam, Sphyncus developed an entirely new set of eccentricities to suit her new surroundings. She took to laying at the top of the stairs and staring down at the action below for extended periods of time. Like a silent guardian, Sphyncus watched over her kingdom from on high at all hours of the day. If for some reason the bedroom door at the top was shut she'd lay across the highest step like a sentinel protecting some forbidden entryway.

If E and Chew were barking at something out the window downstairs, Sphyncus would spring to life and growl the whole way down the staircase before exploding at the window. She didn't yet know why she was mad, she just knew that she was. She seemed to need the entire length of the staircase to rev up her throat before she could fling barks like lightning bolts at whatever was outside.

To everyone's amusement, Sphyncus' growls had somehow taken on a Macho Man Randy Savage quality. "Oh yeah, oh yeah, oh yeah," she'd gurgle to all the challengers outside of the window. Chewie would howl, E-Style would let out her high pitched "byooos!" and the Macho Man would bring the flying elbow drop down from the top of the staircase in the most asinine display of Macho Madness ever witnessed.

The door that led out to the backyard has a screen door that Sphyncus plowed over the first time it was closed. In her defense, she'd never seen one before and she didn't see it that first time, either. She looked like a cop in a bad action movie kicking a door down to get to the perpetrators inside, but in this case the perps were birds chirping and Sheriff Sphyncus had to let them know this town wasn't big enough for the both of them. Hearing birds chirping and running like mad to chase them off became a daily occurrence in the house.

I could be sitting at the table on the back porch with the screen door shut and hear the familiar sound of toenails approaching across the wood floor. Logic says that Sphyncus wanted outside, but since she's never been interested in logic, when I would open the door to let her out she would retreat back into the house. I'd sit there scratching my head for a few minutes wondering what it was all about, then she would come back and do it again. Repeatedly. The house made her weirder and weirder.

Having a yard for the first time, Sphyncus took to digging her nose in the loose dirt of the flower garden then rolling around in it. Her snow shovel nose was just as effective at tilling soil. She ran suicide sprints back and forth in the small strip of grass, stopping randomly to stick her nose up to the knot holes in the wooden fence because apparently, she can get a better sniff of the air like that. When she wasn't running she was just standing around, sniffing the air.

She sunbathed on the concrete with E-Style while Chewie watched from the shade. All three would crowd around me when I sat outside to read. We could even give Sphyncus baths with a hose rather than having to fight for our lives against her in a bathtub.

Best of all, in a house that big there were plenty of new Batcaves for her to crawl under for absolutely no reason at all. We never had a dining table at our apartment, but mom brought one along to the house. The table and all 4 chairs were new obstacles for Sphyncus to military crawl under when going from room to room. When she would hear the garage door raise, rather than just running straight to the house door, she would take a detour through the kitchen. She would then go up next to the wall and slide down onto the floor to slither under a chair and crawl. It makes no sense at all, but she does it almost every single time.

If you go straight ahead at the bottom of the stairs, the door leads into our living room. The couch was placed about five feet inside the door so it was perfect for Sphyncus to get a full running start down the steps before leaping over the side onto it. One time, the laptop computer was sitting there opened up and Sphyncus landed directly on it, sending keys exploding all across the room. Another time she landed directly on Randi as she napped. Sometimes she would hit the slick floor and lose her footing, sending her face first into the arm of the couch.

The first year we spent together in the house was probably the favorite year of my life. It wasn't without its bumps, but overall life was good that year. Having all five of the animals together in a place that size was great to come home to every day. They had constant attention. The cats and the Hogs didn't seem to mind each other much and they had more room than ever before to scatter if they needed to separate. They all loved being able to hang out in a secure place outside. It was all the positive things we hoped it could be.

I was particularly happy that I was able to share all the special places Sphyncus and I had been walking the last three years in the neighborhood with E-Style and Chewie. Sphync and I had walking routines established that consisted of open fields, nature trails, disc golf courses, dried out creek beds, playgrounds, school campuses, and spots in the woods. They were specific and personal to the two of us on our walks, but I was excited to bring E and Chew into the mix and form a little pack. I was never happier than that year with those three at my side.

Throughout 2014 David, Megan, and I started talking about traveling together again. It had been four years since the three of us went on that fateful European trip that ended in Cairo. Despite other trips with different groups, the three of us had a special bond from that trip and everything that resulted from it. We settled on Asia, covering some combination of China and a few other countries to be decided later.

As the plans advanced David started to get a little iffy about it and eventually had to back out due to school, money, and time, which were the same things that had prevented Megan from going to South America with us two years earlier. He tried suggesting something shorter and less expensive, such as a cruise, but Megan had her heart set on seeing China. We didn't want to leave David behind, but everything had been China or bust up to that point, so it quickly got messy. During all the debate about what we should do, I blurted out that if we didn't go to Asia I had no interest in anything else and I was going back to Cairo to visit ESMA.

They were both a little shocked at that, seeing as how Egypt had ripped my heart out the first time, and I shocked myself as well. It was the first time I had ever considered going back and it just shot out of my mouth. As soon as I said it, though, it all made sense. I had a lot of money saved up for China and I wasn't going to settle for something half-assed like a cruise. The money could be put to better use visiting the people that changed my life and helping them out in some way.

I was still in regular contact with Mona and some others from ESMA. There was a debt I always felt I needed to repay for them taking the chance on me and saving Sphyncus. Up to that point the only things I had done to help them out were donating small amounts of money each month and spreading their work through social media to raise awareness.

The only exception was in the spring of 2013 when some friends of mine entered a MoFilm contest for Purina dog food and asked me to be in it with Sphyncus. It was a one minute long condensed retelling of how we met and how much she had changed our lives in a positive way. We didn't win the contest, but they paid me $500 to do it and I gave it all to ESMA. I didn't feel my debt was repaid, but it was a start.

The idea of going back to Cairo spoke a lot to how much my feelings had changed in the last four years. If I could go back and volunteer for them, help at the shelter, and meet the people that had changed my life, maybe then I'd feel like we were even. After a couple of months weighing all the options, Megan and I eventually booked a trip for October and November to China, Cambodia, and Japan. We had an incredible journey together and I felt on top of the world when we got home. 2014 was almost over and it had been a fantastic year.

## Chapter 20

About two weeks after returning from Asia everything changed. Friday night, November 21st, 2014 I got a call from my friend Jon Bratcher in the middle of the night, telling me one of my best friends had been killed by a drunk driver.

Jeremy Pryor was somebody I had known for 17 years. We had been in several bands together the first decade of our friendship. After the last one dissolved in 2007, we decided that for the sake of our friendship maybe we shouldn't play music together anymore as we had drastically different ideas on what good music is and should be. We remained close friends and spoke often about one day, when we were older, setting our differing opinions aside to play music together again. We never got the chance.

I'd be lying if I said we hadn't drifted apart somewhat by the time he died, but we always loved each other as brothers and his death was devastating to me. I had butted heads with him more than anyone I've ever known, but it changed nothing about how we felt about each other. There were countless unresolved regrets that I had to face living with for the rest of my life.

The Red Hot Chili Peppers have a song called "Transcending" with a line that says "a part of me left that only you knew will never be understood." That's how I felt when I tried to come to terms with the fact my friend Jeremy was never coming back. It was the start of a downward spiral for me that took years to recover from. I leaned on the Hogs more than ever to help cope.

Two months after Jeremy died we took E-Style and Chewie in together for their annual vet appointments. E had lost a couple of pounds for the second year in a row and as a small aging dog it was cause for concern. The vet ran some bloodwork on her and the results came back--she was in the early stages of kidney failure.

If anyone out there has ever been through something like that then you know how brutal it is. You fight a battle every single day that you know you're ultimately going to lose. There's only so much that can be done to comfortably prolong an animal's life. At a certain point you have to accept what's happening and make peace with it.

Still, in the midst of the depression from the loss of Jeremy, I emotionally wilted even further with E's diagnosis. Knowing I would only have all three of them for a limited amount of time made the weight of everything I was going through even heavier. The feeling of exuberance I felt toward life after coming home from Asia just two months earlier was gone. The first year in that house that I had dubbed "my favorite year of my life" was over.

For the first little bit nothing changed. E-Style was the same happy old girl she had always been. A couple of months later, we changed her diet permanently to food for renal failure dogs, but she wasn't a fan of it. One thing I can say about my three Hogs is they are the pickiest eaters on Earth. It was hard to get her to eat sometimes, but Sphyncus and Chewie were infatuated with the renal food. It was new and they weren't supposed to have it, therefore they obsessed over it.

Sphyncus didn't want her tasty normal food that was undoubtedly loaded with salt and other flavorful things, but she salivated over that bland renal food. Like all things Sphyncus, there just wasn't logic to be found in her behavior.

Not long after that, I visited Smitty up in northern Virginia and he took me to a float tank. He had been frequenting one and was pleased with the results so he thought it might help me work through the dark place I was in. Floating in the water in the pitch black, drifting further and further into my mind, I searched for peace and something to grasp onto in order to start climbing out of the funk I was mired in.

Jeremy was gone and there was nothing I could do. I had to let him go and take solace in the friendship we had for almost two decades. E-Style hadn't even started to show symptoms of kidney failure, but I was already mourning her. I had to stop and appreciate what we still had left in front of us. I vowed to make every day count from then on.

That May marked five years from when I had first traveled to Egypt. On the actual anniversary date, I wrote a Throwback Thursday post on Facebook about Sphyncus, essentially a very abbreviated version of the first half of this book. It was only a few pages and very basic. I ended it at the part where I walked away from her to go back into the hotel in Cairo without any resolution other than saying I needed to get off the computer and go walk the dog.

I don't really know why I did it. I guess because it was five years and as humans we gravitate toward landmark anniversaries. Part of me just needed something positive to reflect on amidst all the negativity I had been feeling for almost 6 months, to feel like I had done something good. I shared the story to the ESMA Facebook page as well as Mona's, then shut the computer down to take Sphyncus for a walk.

Like all dog walkers, I'll reluctantly admit that I can often be found walking with a leash in one hand and my phone in the other. Notification after notification started blowing up my phone. My little random afternoon musings of Sphyncus's origin story took off and people wanted to know what happened next. Friend requests were coming in from all over the world followed by messages and demands that I finish the story. Previously, I had a decent number of online Egyptian connections, but that day I couldn't keep up with everyone reaching out to me. It somehow went global among animal rescue groups in the span of a few hours.

It took me three weeks, but I did eventually finish the story. Like the first part, it was very condensed and simplified. A few pages and nothing more. It was good enough to placate the masses of fans we had suddenly garnered and I made a lot of new friends in the process. I concluded that the only logical next step would be to make good on my idea from a year earlier and return to Cairo to visit ESMA. I just didn't know when I was going to be able to do it.

A few months earlier Smitty had adopted a dog, Tala, and he brought her to Bowling Green that June to visit. Tala was only about 6 months old but was already the same size as Sphyncus. Given Sphyncus's unpredictability with other animals, we were all worried about how it would go. After about a day of uneasiness, Sphyncus really took a liking to Tala. She was the first dog I'd ever seen her play with in five years and they played nonstop the rest of the time they were in town. They played so much it almost got annoying. It was like having two horses running around the house for a week, growling and running into everything. Circling the kitchen counter, leaping off couches, barreling down the stairs—it just never stopped. Sphyncus had her first real dog friend.

As the summer rolled by, I held on tight to every passing day because I didn't know what the future held for E-Style. It was a good summer with lots of sunbathing and having fun with my power trio. Lots of hanging out in the backyard and going on little excursions when the heat wasn't so bad. E's health stayed steady until sometime around October when she started to slow down a little bit and was getting harder to feed.

The two things you monitor closely with kidney failure are creatinine and BUN levels. Without getting into specifics, they indicate how well the kidney is functioning and how much toxicity is building up. By this time E's were elevating little by little and the effects were becoming more noticeable.

That Halloween I decided it was now or never on an idea that had been lingering around and growing since about 2009. I dressed up as Luke Skywalker from The Empire Strikes Back when he was on Dagobah and E-Style was dressed as Yoda riding around in my backpack. Chewie was an Ewok and Sphyncus was an X-Wing pilot. We entered a Halloween contest held on the downtown square and, much to my surprise, the three amigos kept their cool around all the other animals. I was so proud that day. We didn't even place in the contest, but I still felt great about it. Our costumes were hilarious and totally original. It was a small dream I talked about for years and I finally saw it through. Whatever happened after that, the memory would be there, and I wouldn't have any regrets about it.

As spring came on, E-Style's health continued to steadily decline. She had been going through mitral valve disease (heart failure) since 2012. Because of that, the vets hadn't approved of administering the subcutaneous fluids normally associated with kidney failure treatment. Since it was the only form of treatment we weren't using, I told them I was going to stop bringing her in for bloodwork every month because it only stressed me out watching it get worse and if we couldn't eventually do the fluids then it was pointless. No need to keep spending the money and putting E through it all if there wasn't a magic number we were watching for that would change things. Shortly after that, I got a call back saying that we would begin the fluids at a dosage of 100 ml every other day to see how she responded. I was elated and for the first time in a long time, E-Style actually improved a little bit.

It took a bit of adapting on our end to stick a needle in her back and hold it there for ten minutes. All the bags and tubes hanging up alongside pouches of needles made it feel like we were running a clinic in the house. Of course with a disease like kidney failure, the improvement was only temporary and it wouldn't be long before we had our first scare that we were going to lose her.

On a Sunday afternoon, Randi and I took the Hogs to a nature trail to run around and noticed that E was standing around looking lethargic and confused most of the time. I ended up carrying her the rest of the way and when we came home she looked even worse. She didn't eat anything all day, so we started to get concerned she had taken the inevitable "turn." The next day everything was the same, no energy, no interest in food. It was like she was giving up. We talked to the vet and he said if it continued for another day or two we'd have to bring her in and talk about things. I bawled like a baby at the thought of it. I wasn't ready for that. None of us were. The diagnosis came down about 16 months prior, but everything seemed to suddenly happen so fast.

My sister, Stephanie, is a photographer and called asking if I wanted to do a photo shoot with E-Style the next day, just in case. About a month after I got E in 2001 there was a photo taken of me in the front yard wearing a ZZ Top baseball style shirt holding her up by my chest. Our hair was blowing in the wind and we looked so innocent. Our father/daughter relationship was just beginning. Seven years later, when my mom and stepdad divorced, I took another picture wearing the same shirt holding her up again in the yard before the house sold. 5 years later in 2013, I did it again in a different yard. Same shirt, same pose. It became an annual tradition on her birthday after that. When my sister called to set up a session with E-Style there was only one logical thing I could wear.

*Baladi*

Steph had several locations in mind, so she drove while I sat in the passenger seat with E and mom rode along in the back. I had the window down and the little Bean kept trying to put her head out like she so loved to do. I was reminded of pictures I'd seen online titled "Old Dog's Last Ride" as they were on their way to the vet to have the dog put down because some incurable illness had taken hold.

We went back to the house I grew up in and since nobody was home we posed for pictures in the front yard again like we had first done over 14 years earlier. It was tough to keep my composure. A little while later at a different spot I was laying on the ground with E stretched out across my chest. She laid her head down on my shoulder and I lost it. Almost 15 years of those moments rushed through my mind and I knew I only had so many left. Stephanie later told me it was one of her most difficult moments as a photographer to watch her older brother laying on the ground crying while clutching his dying dog.

When we got back home my cousin, Garrett, came over to say what could possibly be his final goodbye to E. Having lost one of his own dogs suddenly to cancer a couple of years before, he knew what we were going through and gave me some of the best advice I've ever received.

"Every day, tell her everything you want to tell her. Don't leave anything behind in case you don't get another chance. You don't want any regrets with this. Tell her everything you want her to hear."

After he left I called the vet to ask them if they had any ideas at all on anything I could try to get E to eat. It was nearing the end of day 3 and I knew day 4 would mean trouble. He advised we begin giving her the fluids every day from that point on as the kidney was in more trouble than the heart and we should try temporarily giving her things like sandwich meat to entice her to eat.

Miraculously it worked. That night E-Style ate several pieces of sliced turkey. We felt optimistic for the first time in days. Before going to bed I heeded Garrett's advice and had a short conversation with her. I finished with what I would end up saying to her every night after that.

"Horse, I love you forever. I'll see you in the morning. And if I don't then that's okay, I'll see you again. I promise." Followed by a kiss on the head.

The next afternoon she ate some more and by Thursday she was almost back to normal. After three days of thinking she had given up on life, E battled back. She ended up taking a short walk with us and my mind was blown. None of it made any sense. A few people warned us that it could be the infamous "last hurrah" some animals do right before cashing in, but I didn't want to believe it. Seeing her trotting around again like that after days of being at death's door I couldn't accept that it was going to crash down again.

I did some detective work and discovered that Saturday evening, the night before it all started, mom had made some type of beef stew that had onion in the broth. E had been refusing to eat so she put a little on her food to entice her. Obviously, Chew and Sphyncus got some as well. Onions are highly toxic to dogs, especially one who's kidneys were struggling to process things. Sphyncus, being the hardened street mongrel that she is, was unaffected by it but Chewie had a little diarrhea those few days E was so down. We had initially chalked it up to him sensing what was going on with E and getting sick over it because he's always been a nervous dog with an easily upset stomach.

Mom felt horrible and I was shocked she could casually make that mistake but rather than make a scene about it I wanted everyone to learn from it and be more cautious in the future. E-Style survived it, that's what mattered most.

Throughout May and early June, E held on without a lot of changes. She was eating mostly baby food by then, but she was at least eating every day. When it started to get hotter around the beginning of July we noticed her beginning to do a little twitching motion when exposed to the heat for extended lengths of time. After a few minutes her little body would spasm and she'd have to go back in. It broke my heart knowing it was her last summer and she couldn't fully enjoy it.

In addition to her kidneys getting worse, E's dry eye problem had come back to haunt her one last time. She took drops for it every day that kept it at bay for years but suddenly it was an issue again. Little by little her body and immune system were breaking down on her.

I spent August making the most of the Hogs as a power trio. We took them out a lot even though E had to be carried most of the time. We made sure somebody was home with them at all times. Everyone in the house made sacrifices to be there more than normal.

I kept waiting for signs of end stage kidney failure but I never saw them. There was occasional diarrhea but nothing consistent. No vomiting. Her legs got wobbly as she lost weight, but she never lost use of them. She continued to eat baby food although it did get harder and harder to feed her and she progressively ate less as the days went by.

About a week into September she started doing an odd breathing thing that had me worried. She wasn't gasping for air like when her heart acted up, it was more like snoring but while she was wide awake. There wasn't a struggle, it was just really noisy as if she was incredibly congested. I took her to the vet and all they said was the kidneys were getting worse and to just keep doing what we were doing. There was nothing to be done about it. I wanted answers and that was not satisfactory. We'd come so far, I wasn't going to accept that it was just going to remain that way until she died.

A week later I took her to a different vet for a second opinion. It was the first time bloodwork had been run in almost 6 months, since we started the fluids. Her BUN and creatinine were high but not through the roof. The vet sat me down and just kept apologizing over and over. She said the breathing issue was caused by toxins building up and her body was shutting down. I was about to cry and she looked at me helpless. Vets must deal with that situation every single day, but she wasn't numb to it. I pleaded with her to give me an estimated timeframe and after some resistance she laid it on me: One month, maybe two.

I clutched E to my body and paid the bill. It took a while to get my head on straight in the parking lot before I could drive. I'm an ugly crier, I do it easily, and I'm not ashamed of it. One of the costs of having a big heart is wearing it on your sleeve. Countless times in my life I wished I could be somebody else. Somebody stronger and harder. A manly man that chokes it back when times get tough. It would save me a lot of pain. We finally drove home, and I delivered the news to mom and Randi.

Fifteen days later E-Style was gone. She went in her sleep, laying next to mom and Chewie, sometime between midnight and 2 a.m. on September 25th, 2016. We had feared having to make any type of decision, but E-Style gave us one last gift and spared us.

She had her dignity all the way to the end. She never lost control of her bodily functions and she still stood on her own 4 feet. She ate a mixture of sweet potatoes and beets just a few hours before she died.

Her last day on Earth E-Style spent the afternoon with mom while Randi and I went with our friend Chris to get pumpkins to carve. Once we got home mom went out with her boyfriend, so we stayed in for the night watching movies. Randi held E curled up in a blanket throughout the evening. After she went to bed I stayed up with the Hogs until mom got home. I laid on the couch with E, her body pressed up against mine as I played with her hair and feet until we fell asleep. Mom got home around 11 so I scooped E-Style up and carried her to mom's bed while she was in the bathroom. I sat her down, put a blanket over her, and kissed her head.

"Horse, I love you forever. I'll see you in the morning. And if I don't then that's okay, I'll see you again. I promise."

## Chapter 21

I was hollow. The shell of my former self was walking around, living a different life in a different world with little emotion towards anything. I sat on the verge of turning 35 trying to remember what it was like to be a 19 year-old and not have E-Style in my life. I no longer knew who I was or who I was supposed to be. What little relief I had knowing she was no longer in pain was overshadowed by the emptiness my universe had become.

In the time shortly after E-Style's death, Chewie and Sphyncus both attempted to fill her void by cuddling us like they never had before. They even finally sort of bonded with each other. We had always worried Chewie would follow shortly after E because of how tight-knit they were, but the little guy surprised us. Dogs always adapt and, though I wouldn't say Chewie thrived, after a little while of looking lost he seemed to be getting on okay. I was proud of him. He accepted Sphyncus more than he had in the previous 6 years. They became a new tag-team to replace the power trio of old.

Sphyncus's personality changed a bit as well. She laid closer to us, took to sleeping in the bed more often, and even started sunbathing alone. She had previously only sunbathed with E-Style. She knew we were sad and did her best to comfort us. I'd never seen that side of her before. E-Style was the emotionally intelligent dog and somehow Sphyncus seemed to inherit a few of E's traits after she passed on. It helped in the mourning process, but nothing was ever going to be the same.

Once E-Style was gone, I knew it was time to finally go back to Cairo. No more excuses, nothing holding me back. I'd miss the old girl forever, but I had to find something to help me move forward. It had been close to two years since my depression started with Jeremy dying and I couldn't keep living that way. I put out some feelers on Facebook to my Egyptian friends to see what they thought about me coming over. It was unanimous that I should wait until the spring when the weather is relatively mild. Solid reasoning for sure, but it was October--the spring felt like an eternity from then and I was desperate to start turning my life around.

That Christmas, Randi commissioned my friend Matt Simone to paint a piece of the two of us with all five of the animals. When I first laid eyes on it I felt weak. Set in the woods, in the foreground was Bengal peaking up from the bottom with the Hogs standing behind her. Randi was seated on a rock with Chewy cat beside her. I stood behind it all. It perfectly captured those few years we had together in the house, especially the first year when everything had gone so well. My favorite time in my life. Our little family immortalized on canvas. It's one of my most prized possessions.

We took a trip to Prague in January and, as magical as the place is, I never really felt happy the entire time. It felt like I was trying to force myself back into my old life of traveling and experiencing new things, but that person no longer existed. The things that excited me before did nothing but remind me of what felt like a past life.

Shortly after returning from Prague, things hit a new rock bottom. Randi told me she planned to move away from Bowling Green when she graduated in December. She would start applying for jobs all over the country a couple of months before graduation and take the best offer. "If you don't want to come with me then you need to start preparing for me to leave."

I hate to use the word 'betrayal' because that implies some sort of malicious intent. Maybe 'abandoned' would be better. At my absolute lowest point, this is what happened. We had a lot of discussions about what moving away would mean and how it would change everything in our lives. I enjoyed my career in television and there was no guarantee there would be a job opportunity in whatever city she ended up in. I had no interest in starting a completely new career path at age 35 and no interest in going back to school. More importantly, I'm a musician and that will never change. It defines my identity as much as anything else.

I could always try my luck in a new city and hope to find people to play with, but with Randi starting fresh in her new career we had no idea where she'd end up. It would most likely be some small town for a while until she could move up and that would leave me sitting in a room of music equipment alone. When you're in a depression like the one I was in, there's no place for optimism. I loved the bands I was in and the people I had spent decades playing with. It didn't matter whether or not there was ever a possible future for me with music as a career. It's one of the only things that has always made me happy and my lone creative outlet. At this point in my life I needed music more than ever.

After much deliberation, I said no to moving away. For the next few months she tried to convince me to go and I tried to convince her to stay. We both lost. December was still a long time away but I wasn't going to change my mind. That only seemed to strengthen her resolve in staying the course she had plotted for herself. Things were said that could never be taken back and we both realized our paths were no longer intertwined. Maybe my years-long slide into darkness played a role in pushing her away. I can't really say.

She wasn't happy with our lives anymore and wanted to start completely over. I felt more lost and alone than ever before and the idea of leaving everything else behind felt like the wrong move. I guess it speaks volumes about our relationship that she would be willing to move away without me and that I'd be willing to let her. After ten years together, my relationship was now dying a slow, painful death. The person I had spent a decade of my life with would be moving on.

I reached out to Mona about coming to Egypt and she told me of the pending 10-year anniversary celebration for ESMA. There wasn't a solid date locked in yet, but it would most likely be in April or May. I was thrilled at the prospect of being there to witness and take part in something so monumental. A decade of ESMA saving the animals of Egypt was truly something to celebrate. In my mind, I wasn't necessarily worthy of being included, but as soon as Mona mentioned it something inside me clicked. Finally visiting ESMA after so many years was like a light in the dark, showing me the way out. I had to be there.

I volunteered to be a flight parent but didn't know what steps needed to be taken, so that placed the entire situation in Mona's hands. I couldn't book just any flight, it had to be on a specific airline that could accommodate numerous dogs flying back with me on dates coordinated with an animal rescue in America.

March came and went. Then April. I messaged Mona every week or so asking her for updates. It felt like seven years earlier checking in on what was going on with Sphyncus when she was still in their care. I knew I was probably nagging but I couldn't book anything until she told me what to do. I had to be back by May 24th to watch the Hogs while mom went out of town and it was getting closer.

Once we got into May I started to get uneasy. I hadn't heard a word from Mona in a few weeks. On Saturday night May 6th I made up my mind that I could no longer go and that I'd message Mona in the morning to tell her I was sorry, we'd have to try later in the year. I chalked it up to just another thing going badly in my two-and-a half-year streak of unfortunate events.

The next morning I logged into Facebook to send out the bad news only to find that Mona had sent me a message overnight. It was a flight path fully laid out, departing in exactly one week from Chicago and coming back eight days later. The ESMA anniversary would be celebrated on the Friday of that week. She apologized for the delay and asked if it was still okay.

I sat there dumbfounded. I was minutes away from backing out and now this. It took me all of ten seconds of contemplation before making up my mind.

# Baladi

When I booked the flight, hitting 'enter' on the keyboard felt like a fresh start to living. The dark clouds hanging over my head started to break apart at the push of a button. After so many years of repeatedly putting it off, I had just confirmed my return to Egypt. I told her my plan was to come over and do whatever I could to help out and meet as many people as possible. "Put me to work," I said. She agreed and said they'd book the crates for me to fly seven dogs back to the USA.

"You won't just be saving those seven dogs, it means we will have room for seven more. Fourteen dogs will be given a new chance at life." Hard to argue with that. I wanted to make a difference and that would certainly do it. A very nervous excitement overcame me. It was all happening. It was the best I'd felt in years and I hadn't even left yet.

The next step was finding a place to stay. I ended up going with an Airbnb called Pyramids Loft. It was directly across the street from the Pyramids with an amazing view from the rooftop. For a price of under $20 a night it was impossible to say no. Mona wasn't crazy about it as it is right by the stables for the camels and donkeys that are used for tourists around the Pyramids.

"A place of heartbreak for ESMA during the 2011 revolution," she said. I wondered if my camel scammers from 2010 were holed up there somewhere. She attempted to talk me into staying at a resort that wasn't much more expensive than the Loft, but I couldn't be swayed. There was something about the vibe of the place and the people that ran it combined with a rooftop view that couldn't be beat. Three days before checking in I booked it.

Josh Hines

Exactly seven years to the day from the first time I saw Sphyncus hobbling around in the dirt outside of the HUSA Pyramids, I boarded my flight to go back. There was a sense of fate to it. I was about to make my return to the one place in the world I swore I'd never go back to.

## Chapter 22

The back cabin of the plane was almost completely empty. I was seated in the small row on the right side, so I turned left and took a picture of the entirely empty middle row next to me. I posted it to Facebook with the caption "Is this real life? I'm going to stretch out across 5 rows."

Not even a minute later I had a message come through from my friend Kris Shultz. "Lol. I thought that was you across from me!" I looked across the empty seats to see a woman sitting all the way on the opposite side smiling at me.

Like many people I've connected with through Sphyncus, Kris and I had been Facebook friends for a couple of years but had never met in person. She was also headed to Cairo for ESMA's anniversary and had coordinated with the rescue group I would be delivering the dogs to on my flight home. That feeling of fate crept up inside me again. What were the odds that we were on the same flight in the same row? Everything about the journey back to Cairo felt like it was meant to happen.

The plane soon filled up, preventing me from moving over next to her. Once we landed in Vienna for the layover we saw we were on the same flight again to Cairo, so we had a bit of time to hang out together at the airport. I was nervous about being a flight parent, so I had a lot of questions and Kris had a lot of answers. It was her 7th solo trip to Cairo and she had brought dogs and cats back with her every time. She assured me the process was very simple and I really wouldn't even have to do much. I would arrive at the airport with somebody from ESMA and they'd take care of checking in all of the dogs. They'd give me the paperwork and I would merely say they were mine and that was it. I wouldn't see them again until we landed and then I'd just pick them up in baggage claim to meet the rescue group's transporter. It sounded simple enough and set my mind at ease.

When we landed in Cairo, Kris and I made plans to meet up throughout the week to hang out before the ESMA party on Friday. As we exited the airport, the bright sun and hot Egyptian air slapped me in the face like an old spurned lover. We knew each other and at one point had such high hopes for our relationship, but it had all ended so very badly a long time ago. Despite my optimism, I still had very mixed feelings about Cairo. I had been so excited to be there in 2010 only to have everything go so wrong. This was a fresh start, a chance at redemption.

I walked toward the crowd outside and saw a man holding a sign that simply read "ESMA." I smiled in his direction and a small woman next to him motioned for me to follow. The man spoke no English, but the woman filled me in. Her name was Dareen and his was Mohamed. We got into an old gray van and started making our way into Cairo. It was exactly how I remembered it. Chaotic traffic, nonstop car horns, brown every where, and the hot sun above it all.

Dareen and I made small talk throughout the drive and I asked her if we could stop somewhere to buy a phone. Mona had stressed the importance of having a working phone so we could get in touch without me having to be connected to wifi somewhere. It might be hard to believe but it was cheaper to buy a new Samsung phone with unlimited data for a month in Egypt than it was to simply have international data on my existing phone plan.

We stopped in Vodafone and I got my first bit of excitement. A massive argument broke out in the middle of the store between a customer and the workers. Every employee ended up getting involved and eventually the man was forced to leave. The place was small with only two cashier counters, so a line had built up, sending the man into a rage. I laughed about it, but I knew I was partially to blame for it since working out my new phone plan appeared to be a bit of trouble for the representative helping us.

We got back in the van and Dareen asked me if I wanted to go to my room to rest or go see the cat shelter. Hearing the words "cat shelter" initiated a sorely needed second wind. Rest could wait. I was back in Cairo after 7 years. There was no time to waste.

The cat shelter was a three-story building sitting on the corner of a torn up street and a run down alley. "ESMA" was hand-painted in black on the outside wall. The metal doors that opened in the front were loud and reminded me of something you'd see in an old prison. Nevertheless, once those doors were opened I was immediately greeted by barking dogs running at me from every direction. Yes, there was a fleet of dogs at the cat shelter.

I sat down on the steps and let them sniff and lick all over me. One small black dog named Tina was especially friendly, climbing right up in my lap. There was another towards the back of the room that looked like a fat puppy version of Sphyncus. I was in love.

Dareen introduced me to a woman named Nermen who was one of the managers. We hadn't previously known each other online, but she was very welcoming. I was informed that I'd be coming back to the cat shelter the next day and would report to Nermen for job duties.

We ascended a stone staircase up to the second floor where I was greeted by two more dogs. The first was big with long, light brown hair and was very friendly. I later learned his name was Rocky. The second was very timid and looked a lot like Sphyncus if she had floppy ears. She smiled nervously like Sphyncus does, but wouldn't let me pet her. Her name was Assami and it instantly became my goal to befriend that dog before my time at the cat shelter was over.

We passed a room to the right that had more dogs in it. I was on the second floor of the cat shelter but had yet to see any cats. Turning down the hallway, we opened another door and now there were cats everywhere. Two rooms to the left and one straight ahead, all with big glass windows looking in from the hall and big glass windows looking outside. All full of cats. It wasn't overcrowded, but they certainly had their share of felines roaming around.

Dareen led me to the room at the end of the hall. There was a woman casually seated on a mattress smoking a cigarette with a big smile on her face. She was surrounded by cats, enjoying their company as much as they looked to be enjoying hers. It was Bahra Fahmy, one of the founders of ESMA.

Bahra and I had spoken very little over the years. The majority of my direct ESMA contact had always been with Mona. Bahra was really friendly, her English was excellent, and she welcomed me with open arms. Such a drastic change from my first time in Egypt. She had a sort of Western vibe to her and was the first woman I'd met not wearing a hijab. She and Mona were the two main power players of ESMA. The most important people involved in animal rescue in the entire city of Cairo, maybe in all of Egypt. I felt star struck, as if in the presence of royalty.

Next I met Lia Theodoridis. We'd been friends online for about 6 years prior to this but never interacted much. She's from Holland but Lia is very instrumental in helping ESMA with any number of things from fundraising to overseas adoptions. A very take-charge kind of person, she was instructing some of the workers on what to do while I spoke with Bahra.

Lia had traveled over from Holland with a woman named Anne-Marie Verhoeven who I was meeting for the first time. I liked her right away. She had short hair dyed bright red, an endearing accent, and instantly started making jokes. It doesn't make any sense, but her accent sounded thicker than Lia's, yet I could somehow understand her better. She had a sweet, playful nature to her that makes you want to talk to her just to hear her voice.

Before leaving the cat shelter, I met Nermen's husband, Mohamed Mido, who is one of ESMA's vets. Again, he was friendly right from the start. I liked him as soon as we shook hands. Everyone at the shelter was so hospitable. Where were these people in 2010 when I needed them? It really goes to show the difference in personality between people who care for animals and those that do not.

Across the alley from the cat shelter was a placed called The Happy Home. It's basically a big room with blankets and pillows all over the floor and dozens of cats running around. Dareen's desk sits in the middle of it all. What an office that must be to come to work to every day.

The cats were incredibly friendly, so I sat down on the floor to play with them. Several started climbing on me, sitting in my lap, and pawing my pants. Dareen took my phone and snapped some pictures. When she handed it back, I looked at the pictures and hardly recognized the face looking back at me. Grinning from ear to ear with eyes lit up. A man who was loving life. I hadn't seen him in years. It hit me that I hadn't stopped smiling the entire time I'd been in Cairo. Whatever nerves or reservations that existed in my subconscious had disappeared as soon as I sat down in the van with Dareen and Mohamed.

Eventually fatigue started to set in. I needed some rest if I was going to survive whatever work was in store for me the rest of the week. I'd been up for close to 30 hours and it was beginning to hit me.

I got into Dareen's car and was in awe of her calm demeanor while navigating the legendary chaotic Cairo traffic. When we got closer to the hotel, the Pyramids came into view off in the distance. The sky was dark blue, and they looked like black triangles posturing over the city. Even though I'd seen them before they were just as majestic the second time, even in the dark.

Dareen looked uncomfortable dropping me off at Pyramids Loft. We were in a short, narrow alley that appeared to be lifeless other than the sounds of baladi dogs barking somewhere in the vicinity. To the left was a row of rundown buildings and to the right stood a small wall separating us from the Giza Plateau. She clearly didn't approve of my lodging choice any more than Mona had. I didn't care. The Pyramids were literally across the street, I'd visited the ESMA cat shelter and met people I considered heroes. I reassured her numerous times that I was fine and she returned the favor by reassuring me repeatedly that Mohamed would be picking me up at 10 A.M.

With that, Dareen nodded and gave me a nervous smile as she drove off. I started to make my way down a dirt path between some buildings and stables. Halfway down I saw a big metal door with a sign saying Pyramids Loft. I used the buzzer on the wall and the owner, Thomas, came down to greet me. He led me up to the roof and handed me some hot tea that tasted unlike anything I'd ever had before.

Sitting on the roof drinking tea with the Pyramids a mere stone's throw away, I felt something strange. I couldn't identify it at first as it had been such a long time since I last felt it, but after a few minutes I could no longer deny it. Peace. Something inside me knew that the next 6 days were going to have a profound effect on my life going forward.

## Chapter 23

Despite having been up for a day and a half, I didn't sleep well that first night. My room had no air conditioning, just a ceiling fan on full blast and a window. It also didn't have a bathroom. I had to exit into a common area then go down a hall to one of the two shared bathrooms. When you get up to pee as often as I do in the night, it becomes a pain in the ass and it wakes you up a bit more each time.

A little before 10 A.M., I walked down the dirt path to the alley where Dareen had dropped me off and took a seat on a stone ledge to wait for Mohamed. I sat there for about 20 minutes before various taxi drivers and men with camels started hitting me up for rides. It took multiple 'la shukrans' before they let me be. Sometime around 11, Mohamed rolled up in the van an hour late. It would become our daily routine, each day running behind and unable to communicate with each other verbally to sort it out.

He took me back to the cat shelter where I was greeted by Nermen. She told me I'd be helping a crew clean and paint the second floor of the building. She then asked if I needed to change clothes. I was wearing gray Converse Chucks, old jeans, and a white t-shirt. Nothing special but apparently nicer than she was comfortable with due to the nature of the work I would be doing. I confirmed these were my work clothes and had no problem ruining them. She smirked and said, "As you like." A true Egyptian phrase if there ever was one.

I spent the first couple of hours working with an older woman whom I think was named Abir and two young teenage girls whose names sounded like Aranya and Ermeena. None of them spoke English beyond exchanging names. They showed me the cleaning materials and their methods of using them, then we got to work scraping the tile on the lower part of the walls, washing the windows, and scrubbing the floors in the three cat rooms. There was a lot of smiling and laughing as I tried to figure out what I was supposed to do.

A couple of hours later, a group of guys showed up with bright yellow paint for the walls. None of them spoke any English and I didn't want to look foolish so I watched for a few minutes to see how they were going about it. It was a very crude method of using rollers attached to broken broomsticks. Their accuracy was impressive and they didn't make much of a mess. I, on the other hand, got globs of bright yellow paint all over the floor on my first try. It was embarrassing, and the crew had a good laugh at my expense. A couple of them tried to take the stick back from me but I refused; I had to earn their respect and do my share of the work. I was curious if they knew who I was or why I was there.

The longer the day went the more breaks the guys took. I guess it's the American mentality in me, but I stayed the course working. I didn't go to Egypt to take breaks. I went to work. I don't know if it made them uncomfortable or if they just wanted to integrate me into their group, but they offered me tea and a chair enough times that I finally took it. I didn't want to seem rude and I had come to enjoy their company. I regret not getting any of their names.

Nermen brought us food for lunch and I decided to make my play to befriend Assami, the floppy-eared Sphyncus. Her and Rocky had been in the same hallway as the day before. Every time I went by, she would retreat to a metal shelving unit and stand on the bottom shelf looking out. It was so pitiful and cute.

I offered up chips to both dogs and it took all of 5 seconds for Assami to love me forever. She was all over me from that point on, even when I ran out of food. The rest of the night whenever I'd walk through the hallway I'd say, "Hey, it's the chip man," and she'd wag her tail and run up to me. A lot of the cats and dogs on the second floor got paint on them before the day was over, and Assami ended up with a yellow spot right on her nose. She flashed a smile that looked just like Sphyncus and, with that paint mark adding to her cuteness, I fell in love. It was dangerously easy to get attached to all the animals I'd been around that day, but her especially.

In the evening, I ventured back downstairs to meet up with Lia and Anne-Marie to discuss ordering food. Everyone was congregating in a big room full of cats toward the back of the building. It's a strange room; the walls were at least 20 feet tall and rather than a proper ceiling, it had some type of thatch roof that resembled a hut.

I sat down on the floor and a white long-haired, one-eyed cat came over. He jumped onto my shoulders and pressed his body up against my head over and over while purring and meowing. If I put him down, he would climb back onto my shoulders and purr in my ear again--obviously a parrot in a past life, but reincarnated as the sweetest cat in Cairo.

I recalled the conversation I had with the woman on the street in 2010. She put her life in danger crossing Haram Street just to try to convince me that the animals of Egypt were dangerous, and nobody wanted them. If she could only see me now and how wrong she was.

My mind drifted over to the kids that had been chasing Sphyncus the day I got her out from under the car. Seven years later, they'd be close to adults. It's possible some of those kids would've been about the same age now as some of the guys I'd been painting with all day. It made me feel conflicted. I had dreamed about doing the impossible and finding those kids so I could rub it in their faces how happy Sphyncus was in America. I wanted to scold them for how poorly they had represented their country and their people. I had wanted to shame them for so long for what they'd done. As I sat there on the floor with that one-eyed cat perched on my shoulder purring in my ear, I just wanted to forgive them.

Because of those kids I had an amazing dog that had changed my life. I was back in Cairo doing good things with good people. They were just kids. They didn't know any better--their parents didn't teach them any better and their society didn't guide them along a better path. The guys I'd befriended that day could have been just like them when they were young, but now they're working to give those animals a better life.

Nermen opened the refrigerator in the lobby to get some medicine out and Lia spotted a black bag inside with fur sticking out of it. She demanded Nermen tell her what it was at once. Nermen explained that a sick cat had died that morning and there was nowhere else to store it. The person that picks up the dead animals to bury them in the desert will only pick them up if they have several. They won't just take one or two all the way out there. Hence, the dead cat being stored in the fridge. Lia didn't seem happy about it, but there wasn't much that could be done. Nermen seemed somewhat embarrassed and sort of glanced around the room to see everyone's reactions. I just stood there not knowing what to make of it all.

Mohamed drove me back to Pyramids Loft and I crashed hard. Though it had been a long day of nonstop work, I felt great. Exhausted but great. I had done something good and helped out. It's what I came to do and there'd be plenty more over the next few days. Busting ass all day for the betterment of others isn't an opportunity I get very often so I cherished it. It was therapeutic.

Sometime in the middle of the night, I was awoken by a rustling sound on the table beside my bed. I jolted awake, thinking maybe I had imagined it, and reached for my phone to shine a light over. Something jumped onto the bed.

I yelled and scrambled to the light switch by the door. An orange cat sat staring back at me from the middle of the bed. I'd left my window open again and it must have come in looking for food. It looked healthy and was remarkably friendly. Maybe it was a hotel cat? I didn't want to chance anything. The last thing I needed was fleas getting on my stuff or the cat peeing on something. I picked it up and set it outside on the window sill and closed the shutters.

*Baladi*

As I was leaving the next morning, I saw the orange cat still on the window sill sleeping peacefully. It made me feel guilty. I went over to pet it and decided if it came in again I'd let it stay. I'd be getting filthy anyway. I had made friends with the little black dog Tina, floppy-eared Assami, and the one-eyed parrot cat. A little orange roommate wouldn't do any harm.

Just like we had done 7 years before, I got up early that day to see the Pyramids. I didn't plan on being a tourist much, but the Pyramids right across the street was something I couldn't pass up. Once again, as soon as I walked through the gate a scammer walked up to offer his tour services. I had told myself I wouldn't get roped in again, but I went ahead and let the guy do his thing. He was friendly, had an excellent mustache, and was at least the tenth person I'd met named Mohamed. No camels were involved, and I really wanted to hear somebody say "sfeenkus" over and over.

The highlight of his personal tour was when he climbed on top of one of the smaller pyramids and encouraged me to follow him up. I took maybe three pictures that weren't worth it before armed guards ran us off. Afterward, like the camel scammers from 2010, he led me somewhere a little secluded and tried to rip me off. I should have expected it, but it was still disappointing. I had every intention of giving him some money, but he got pushy and his demands were a bit over the top.

"My friend, you have something for me now?" he asked holding his hands out.

"Yeah, sure. I got you."

"American money is good, American money is good."

"I don't have any American money."

"Is okay, American money is good."

"What? No, I don't have any. I have pounds." I hadn't been keeping much money on me at all. Opening a wallet full of bills was something I had learned to never do again.

"My friend, some people pay as much as two hundred dollars for this tour today."

"No, they don't."

"Yes, yes. Two hundred dollars."

"Nobody pays you that. How's two hundred pounds sound?" After conversion that was equal to a little over ten dollars.

"My friend, people pay much more than that. Come on, come on," he said rubbing his hands together while scanning the area around us.

"No. That's all I have," I showed him my strategically empty wallet. The rest of my money was simply in my pocket. "Sorry, you cleaned me out."

"This is not much," he said.

"That's more than double what I paid to get in. It's enough." He didn't look happy but accepted there was nothing he could do. I still drastically overpaid him.

I went back to my hotel and changed clothes to wait for Mohamed the driver to pick me up. He said he'd be there at 11 a.m. and it was getting close to time. Around noon, he still hadn't shown up so I called Dareen. Apparently Mohamed is ESMA's only driver and they had him running errands that morning. She told me to just get some rest in the room and he would be there in 45 minutes. I offered to take an Uber but she insisted I wait.

My American brain couldn't comprehend sitting around and resting when I was supposed to be working, especially losing out on two hours of work. I took a half hour nap then waited around some more. Around 1:30, I called Dareen back. Again, she assured me he was on his way and would call when he was getting close.

Around 3 p.m., four hours after scheduled, Dareen called me and said Mohamed was outside. He greeted me with a sheepish smile and drove me back to the cat shelter. It took about half an hour to get there. I felt like I'd lost the majority of the day and was glad I'd made the decision to see the Pyramids earlier, so I wouldn't view my Wednesday in Cairo as a waste.

As the door opened we were greeted by Anne-Marie in the lobby who started right in teasing me about my tardiness. The crew I'd been with the day before had already done the majority of the work, so I just hung around playing with the cats until somebody told me what to do. Eventually I made my way up to the third floor, the one remaining place I hadn't seen at the cat shelter.

Cats, cats, and more cats. All so sweet. Some had obvious ailments—missing an eye, tongue hanging out, skinny, limping. The one thing they all had in common was their desire for human attention.

Nermen came to let me know we'd be taking all of the dogs and putting them in the big room at the back of the shelter with the twenty-foot walls and thatch roof. The dogs mostly hung around the lobby, but there was going to be some renovation work done there so they needed them out of the way.

The bigger problem was the thatch-roof room had long cages that lined the back wall filled with sick and feral cats that also needed to be moved. These cats were so feral you couldn't get near them. They'd been found in horrible conditions on the streets and ESMA was getting them healthy before turning them loose again. After seeing them for myself, I understood that there was no domesticating them. They were wild and fearful and aggressive.

Two of the guys I had worked with the day before got the ominous task of rounding them up into carriers and putting them in different cages in one of the other rooms. That long cage ran the entire length of the back wall and looked to be handmade. It had a wood top and wooden columns with chicken wire on the side. It was tall enough to get inside but you had to hunch over, which is exactly what those guys did. I was to remain outside of the cage and lock the door shut behind them.

Slowly they each went in wielding a stick and cat carrier. As soon as the door shut behind them, the cats went absolutely berzerk. I'd never seen anything like it. They were climbing the sides, flinging themselves everywhere, hissing. Much wilder than I had imagined. Those guys deserved a medal for bravery after trapping themselves in there with them.

One by one they got most of them out before one managed to slip past when the door opened. That crazy cat climbed almost all the way to the top of the wall before sliding back down. One of the guys grabbed it by the scruff of the neck and it went completely nuts. He was barely able to get it into a cage before it tore his arm to shreds. They were all smiles and laughing about it afterward, but I was stunned.

Before the day was over, I really wanted to go say bye to Assami, but I stopped myself. Even though I didn't know if I'd ever see her again, I couldn't let myself get attached since I couldn't take her home with me. I found out months later that she got adopted by a family in England.

At the end of the night, Mohamed drove me back to the Loft and we started using translate apps on our phones to communicate with each other, something we should have been doing all along. He was to pick me up the next morning and take me to the dog shelter for some serious cleaning work. I love cats and enjoyed my time at the cat shelter, but I was most anxious to see the dog shelter. It's where Sphyncus had stayed, and everything I visualized in my head about ESMA took place there.

Shortly after arriving back at my room, Kris Shultz messaged asking if I wanted to meet her and her friend Mohamed El-bebawy out for drinks. Mohamed was around 25 years old and the nephew of one of Kris's best friends in America. Every time she went to Cairo, he would pick her up at the airport and travel around with her everywhere she went. Kris suggested meeting up at a place called Bull's Eye in the Duqqi district close to downtown.

I still hadn't spoken with any of my Egyptian friends that weren't actual ESMA employees, so I needed to get the ball rolling before running out of free nights. Heidi Alsabban is one of my oldest and best friends in Cairo, so I called her first and fortunately she was free on such short notice.

The ride to Bull's Eye was the first in a series of awkward Uber rides that lasted at least an hour in total silence because the driver didn't speak any English. The driver's name was Mohamed, because of course it was, and we listened to the radio the entire duration. I have to admit I actually enjoyed cruising through the crazy Cairo traffic. Not being able to make small talk gave me a lot of time to reflect on the past few days and what was still to come. With my growing fondness for Cairo, the traffic wasn't as intimidating anymore, and I could appreciate the city as we passed through the different neighborhoods.

Kris, Mohamed, Heidi, and I really clicked that night and we formed sort of a little family away from home. It was nice, completely different than anything I had experienced in 2010. All the locals were incredibly inviting and viewed Kris and me as their guests. Throughout the night, we hooked up with one of Kris's acquaintances, Osama, and ended up leaving Bull's Eye to meet one of his friends at a coffee shop. Once it became clear the coffee shop was closing, we left and drove to another restaurant to have more drinks.

At Kris's urging, Mohamed told us a story from her last trip to Cairo. They were together and some type of weasel ran across his foot, terrifying him.

"Tell him that line you told me," Kris said laughing, egging him on.

"He ran across my foot and I yelled. Kris asked what it was, and I said, 'It's Egyptian weasel. They have no bones.'" Kris and I busted into hysterical laughter.

"They feel like jelly going across my foot. They have no bones." He had a completely straight face and was deadly serious about it which made us both laugh even harder.

"What? It's a mammal. It's a weasel, of course it has bones," I said.

Heidi chimed in, "No, they don't have bones."

I was dumbfounded. "You really believe that? Is that a common belief?" I looked at Kris. She just smiled and shrugged back at me.

"I've never looked it up anywhere but everyone I know thinks they have no bones," Heidi said.

Osama jumped in. "It has no bones! It has no bones!"

I admit that a few of us in that group had been drinking so it only made the whole thing funnier, but it was still one of the more outlandish claims I'd ever heard.

Heidi started Googling Egyptian weasels on her phone. "See, it doesn't say anywhere that they have bones."

"Heidi, why would it have to verify that they have bones? It wouldn't say if they do but I'm sure it would say if they didn't." I was still laughing about it.

"It's like the reason I don't like Batman is because he is a bat," Mohamed said. Of course I laughed even harder then. I loved my new friends.

Eventually, I convinced Heidi to sing for us. She had studied music and is an aspiring singer for hire. I had only heard little snippets she would post online so I wanted to hear her in person. Sitting there at the table surrounded by people she really didn't know, Heidi lightly sang mesmerizing Arabic melodies and completely blew us away. It was beautiful.

Around 3 a.m., we decided to call it a night. I was supposed to be picked up by Mohamed the driver at 10 a.m. and even though he'd been late both days so far, I still wanted to be ready just in case. Kris and Mohamed took an Uber together, and Heidi drove Osama and me. It took about an hour to get back to the Loft. The traffic wasn't bad, but Heidi got lost a couple of times.

We ended up on Haram Street, and I started looking around to see if I recognized anything from 2010. Part of me had wanted to visit the HUSA Pyramids and walk through where I had first met Sphyncus. Without her I wouldn't have been back in Cairo or hanging out with any of these people. It would've been nice to see our little spot in the dirt again. Ultimately, we didn't come across it and I didn't want to keep Heidi out driving up and down the street all night, so we headed back to the Lofts and she dropped me off.

Despite how tired I was, my mind was racing. Walking down that dirt path, I felt like I was on a natural high. What a night. What a day. We had practically closed three bars. In Cairo, of all places. What universe was this? Certainly not the same one as 2010. We had changed timelines. This new reality made more sense than the previous one and was filled with much more optimism. The conservative Muslim country had shown me a night out on the town that I didn't even know was possible.

I got to bed a little after 4 and, before I could even fall asleep, I heard the familiar sound of cat feet landing on the floor. Turning on my phone light I saw the little orange cat standing there looking at me. It jumped on the bed, curled up next to my chest, and went to sleep.

Chapter 24

Thursday morning I left the window open for the little orange cat and headed out to meet Mohamed. The dog shelter and a long day of hard work awaited. The road we took was even worse than the others I'd seen in the city. He had to slow to a crawl with the emergency flashers on to cross numerous bumps and potholes. The road leading to the shelter had a stream to the right filled with trash and the embankments on both sides looked like ramps made of garbage.

I can't even imagine how Cairo came to be in such a state and I have no idea how it could ever be repaired. The roads, that stream, the buildings; so many things are in such an awful state. One might think money and time is all it would take but I disagree. It would require a lifestyle change on a societal level. The population would have to change their entire way of thinking and rid themselves of bad habits. Habits that could easily be slipped back into.

It made me sad. Cairo is such an old city, you can see the old beauty still lurking around in places and the potential to attain it again. I hope someday there's an initiative and resources to clean it up. I look forward to visiting that Cairo.

The van stopped next to a large compound. Like the cat shelter, the only identifying feature is "ESMA" hand painted on the entry way wall. The door opened, and we were greeted by yet another man named Mohamed, because of course that would be his name. Mohamed Ibrahim, with a big mustache above an even bigger smile. He spoke no English but would be my boss for the day.

A few of the dogs in the lobby caught my attention right away. The first was unidentifiable--it barely had any hair and looked like it had been burned. A young woman named Karima, who spoke a little English, told me it was a husky that had been set on fire.

I almost wasn't even surprised. Following ESMA online for 7 years, I had seen some atrocities posted on their page. As bad off as the husky was, it didn't even remotely compare to some of the other things they've dealt with. I knelt down and the husky came right up to me to let me scratch the few tufts of hair she still had. A dog with no reason at all to ever trust anyone ever again, let alone a stranger, came over to me for affection. I almost cried right in front of everyone. Who would do such a thing to that sweet, beautiful dog?

There was a black dog walking around with long strips on its front legs and chest completely devoid of hair and skin. You could see muscle and bone in a couple of places. It was absolutely heartbreaking. Unlike the husky, she wasn't friendly. But why would she be? Mohamed and Karima cleaned the wounds and applied some ointment but no bandages. I know in some cases bandages can do more harm than good, but the dog kept licking the wounds so I wasn't sure what good anything was going to do.

Worst of all was a twitching German shepherd laying on its side in a cage alone. I never found out what was wrong with it, but it was clearly dying. Based on videos I'd seen online, I suspected it had either been poisoned or sustained some type of nerve damage from trauma. ESMA is strictly no kill and view situations like that as inshallah. "If Allah wills it." It was hard to see the dog like that knowing it would thrash until its last breath but I understand the mentality behind letting it go out on its own.

We wouldn't put a person down so why do we put an animal down? I know that's controversial and many people don't agree with it, but I see all living things as equals. When E-Style was fading near the end, I posted a few things online about not knowing if I'd be able to let her suffer on the way out. I've never believed in euthanasia, but I couldn't stomach the idea of E having terrible quality of life and being miserable. I was conflicted and not looking forward to possibly making the decision, so I reached out to friends to get different perspectives. Every Egyptian that I heard from all told me to let her go naturally on her own. It's the way it happens in nature and will happen when God wills it. Inshallah.

Mohamed walked me over to a building on the left and handed me a scraper to clean the tile walls and floors. He set a bucket of water and cleaning solution on the floor with a big roll of scourer pads and motioned for me to clean the entire inside of the building.

I was standing in a wide hallway with a big room to the left full of dogs and a doorway to the right leading to two more rooms full of dogs. Most of them were friendly but some were suspicious of me and kept their distance. An audience of wild Sphyncuses barking at my every move.

That was some of the hardest physical work I've ever done in my life. The walls and floors were absolutely disgusting. I spent the next several hours crouched down wearing out my arms scraping who knows what off the walls. The fact that I knew exactly what I was going to be doing at least gave me a goal to work towards. I could break it down in sections in my head to periodically feel like I was making progress.

There was a group of kids and teenagers working in the area as well. They did the majority of the floor cleaning in the building I worked in and cleaned up areas outside. None of them spoke much English, but they all referred to me as Mr. Josh and I loved it.

Just like the crew I worked with at the cat shelter, it triggered memories of 2010 Cairo and the kids I had seen. What a difference between those two sets of boys. 2010 Cairo kids were the scum of the Earth that put effort into beating and torturing a dog while the 2017 Cairo kids were doing hard labor to help a whole shelter of dogs. I admired the kids I worked with that day. They were hard workers and fun to be around. They treated me like one of their own and helped whenever I didn't know what to do, and they always had smiles on their faces.

Before the day was over, I also cleaned a small office building that was being used as their vet clinic. Numerous injured dogs were coming and going while I scrubbed the walls and floors. It's hard to describe my feelings on what I saw that day. Some of the dogs were in rough shape due to whatever circumstances they had been found in, but clearly ESMA was taking as good of care of them as possible with the limited resources they had available. It was both sad and uplifting. Knowing that they had been at the shelter for at least a few days, I could only imagine how bad off they were before arriving there. Seeing Mohamed, Karima, and those kids working so hard all day left me inspired. They had to truly care about what they were doing, and I don't expect they are paid well. It wouldn't surprise me if the kids were volunteering at their parents' request.

I still hadn't seen Mona Khalil yet, but she called me to see how late I was going to be at the shelter as she would be coming by in the evening. Meeting Mona had been one of my highest priorities for years but, unfortunately, it would have to wait a little longer. Mohamed the driver showed up at the dog shelter before her around 5 or 6 and needed to pick me up so he could get back to the cat shelter and run errands for Lia.

We ended up getting stuck at the cat shelter for a while before everyone got their affairs in order. When factoring in the drive times, it had to have been at least 8 p.m. before anybody actually went anywhere. Eventually Bahra called an Uber for us to share.

Having not talked to Bahra much over the years, the ride gave me some good bonding time with her to find out her story. She described her home as a ranch and said she had around 20 or so dogs, countless cats, and even more that lived outside. There's an air about her that says she's seen and been through some bad stuff over the years. Living in Cairo and founding ESMA would leave its emotional scars on a person, and I could tell Bahra had been worn down by it. Still, she worked tirelessly and was quick to react if the situation called for it.

During a slow point in the ride she thought she heard a kitten somewhere outside and wanted to get out to look for it. It genuinely stressed her out when we didn't see one anywhere. There aren't words to accurately state how much respect I have for her and everyone I'd met thus far.

Bahra dropped me off at Pyramids Loft and I got cleaned up for dinner. There's a hookah restaurant right around the corner that I had been itching to eat at since first arriving. It has an outside balcony on the second floor with a perfect view of the Pyramids Light and Sound Show. I had caught glimpses of the show from the roof of the Lofts each night, but I never sat down to watch the entire thing. It didn't seem worth the time. Over the course of a nice dinner seemed like the perfect opportunity to take it in. I ordered a water, mango juice, stuffed grape leaves, and a vegetarian pasta dish that cost around 80 LE (less than $5). Excellent value for a great meal with an amazing view.

If it weren't for the long day of cleaning I probably would have been too excited to sleep. The next day was the reason I had come over: the ESMA 10 Year Anniversary celebration. With the window opened up for my little orange friend to come in whenever it felt compelled to, I laid down and passed out.

Chapter 25

Mohamed the driver was at his most punctual on the morning of the anniversary party. It would be the last time I rode with him. We stopped by the cat shelter to pick up the little black dog, Tina, then got on our way.

Throughout the week, whenever I posted pictures online of what I was up to, a lot of my friends had become invested in Tina, as she was always around. She was Mrs. Personality and several people expressed interest in paying for me to adopt her or adopting her themselves. As it turns out, she was actually Nermen and Mido's dog, but was always at the shelters due to her friendly personality. For the kids that visit that might be afraid of dogs, Tina was the ideal candidate to make them more comfortable.

She sat in my lap looking out the window for the entire ride to the dog shelter and it reminded me of all the years E-Style had done the same. Any other time it would have most likely made me sad or upset, but my mood had been significantly different since landing in Cairo. Rather than Tina making me miss E-Style like I expected, she instead made me appreciate all the times I got to experience a sweet little dog riding in my lap and the opportunity to have it once again. I soaked it up. It felt like healing.

Entering the big metal doors, I was greeted by Dareen, who was holding a little dog and passing out meal vouchers. The dog shelter looked very different from the day before. It was in the early stages of a party. People were everywhere, there were tables with refreshments, Nermen and Mido were selling t-shirts, and speakers were set up for karaoke. Mohamed Ibrahim and the cleaning boys were keeping all the dogs in check. Everybody had roles they were happy to play. Mona had told me she'd be there before me in the morning but, in Egyptian fashion, she still hadn't arrived. In the meantime, Dareen introduced me to an amazing woman named Heidi Tallat.

Heidi is a middle-aged woman from Germany that has lived in Egypt for a long time. Somehow, we had never connected online before and I have no idea how that's possible. She's consistently been an ESMA volunteer involved in activities every single week since the early days and I'd been in contact with dozens of ESMA workers, volunteers, and supporters for 7 years. It made no sense that we hadn't come across each other before. No matter, she's one of the sweetest people I've ever met in my life and her care for the ESMA dogs is next level. She just lights up around the dogs and they all adore her. It's a powerful bond to witness.

While standing there in one of the dog runs with Heidi, I looked up and saw Mona walk in with a small camera crew. After 7 long years, I was going to meet the person that changed my life. The person I traveled all the way to Egypt to see.

Being an American, I walked up with a big smile on my face and started to extend my arms, readying the biggest hug I could muster. Mona stuck her arm straight out for a handshake. Haha! I had to laugh at myself. We shook hands and I must have looked like a total stooge fawning over her.

She led me through a gate into a large dirt lot. Dogs came running up from every direction to greet us and Mona casually dropped bits of each dog's story and how long they'd been there. There were countless holes peppering the dirt that had been dug by the dogs to get out of the sun. As we approached, the very ground itself appeared to give birth to baladis as heads popped out of holes, followed by bodies scrambling out to come say hello. Sweet, genius little dogs everywhere.

Mona led me to the left side of the lot where a series of large runs extended all the way down and wrapped around the back end. They were like large rooms that had fences for walls and about a dozen dogs inside each one. That's where the oldest dogs that had been there the longest were kept. They all came running up to the gates to greet us as we walked by.

I had a long list of questions to ask and Mona was eager to answer them all. The ESMA dog shelter came first and it was founded by Mona, Bahra, Susie Nassar, and Kristen Stilt. I hadn't thought of Kristen in a long time but without her none of this would have happened. In 2017 ESMA housed 536 dogs, 489 cats, and two donkeys, but those numbers have grown significantly since then.

In the ten years ESMA had been open, only two baladi dogs had ever been adopted out within the country. They had adopted out other breeds in Egypt but all of the baladis went to rescues or homes overseas. Egyptians tend to view purebreds as status symbols so they don't want the baladis.

One of the biggest problems ESMA suffers is people calling them to pick up dogs or dropping them off at their door, then disappearing. They promise to sponsor or help with donations then are never heard from again. ESMA can't turn away injured animals so it's constantly more mouths to feed and clinical costs without new money coming in.

We walked along the back, passing more runs of dogs. Around a corner, we went through a big wooden door into another large open dirt lot, a little smaller than the first one. There were more dogs everywhere, all running up to us just like the last group. Mohamed Ibrahim greeted us and started speaking with Mona in Arabic. In one of the most flattering moments of my life, he asked her if he could hire me. I promised I would return to volunteer again and with those words decided there would be a third trip to Cairo in my future. Most likely many more.

We walked across the dirt lot watching out for holes that dogs could pop out of at any second and headed toward another door at the opposite end. There was a donkey standing by the door eating grass and a dog was standing nearby. Mona told me the two were bonded so they couldn't be adopted out. She opened the wooden door and it led to a third, smaller dirt lot. There were a lot less dogs there and they all had obvious ailments, like mange. Another donkey stood directly to the right of the door.

We backtracked to the first main dog area and made our way down the one side we had yet to go down. It was an outdoor hallway of sorts that was lined with small runs that only had a few dogs or single dog in each.

"Many of these dogs can't be around other dogs. I don't like leaving them in there but they can't always be trusted. Like this one." Mona pointed to a big somber dog with its face up by the bars. "He doesn't like other males. He's okay with females but not males.

"Recovering from diarrhea," she said passing by a cage. "This is a great boy. An awesome boy." He looked like a big white pitbull mix with brown spots. "But he just needs to be an only boy. Only pet. He just doesn't like certain dogs. He's great with humans. I hate him being locked in here. We take him out and walk him and everything, but we just can't trust him around the others. His name is Captain," she said.

"Captain," I repeated. I loved some of their names. It didn't surprise me that many of the dogs couldn't be left alone in the open with the others. Sphyncus was like that. Fending for yourself on the streets had to leave every other animal looking like competition. It would make adopting them out harder, but at least they were never at risk of being put down.

Mona walked me over to another door. "They abandoned him at the clinic and did not come back for him. Heracles." He looked like the saddest dog I'd ever seen in my life. Laying at the back of the run with his face down between his paws. He didn't respond to Mona's attempts to get his attention, he just laid there looking depressed. "He is big and had leg issues and couldn't walk. Now he walks and stands."

As we passed door after door, it was more of the same story. They were trying to get the dogs used to other dogs. Earlier I had seen a few minor skirmishes break out in the first dirt lot that went far enough several workers had to separate the dogs involved. It was unfortunate because probably 99% of the people compassionate enough to want one of the ESMA dogs most likely already have other dogs. You'd have to be a dog lover to go through the trouble of adopting one and flying them overseas.

Mohamed Ibrahim was now with us and he opened a cage door letting out two calm, perfectly healthy looking dogs. One was blonde and the other was copper, both looked like a lab mix of some kind. Mona spoke: "An American theater professor was visiting Cairo, the American University of Cairo, and she found those two. She said she didn't want to take them in until she managed to prepare something for them and then she disappeared. We took them in, we've been writing to her 'do you want the dogs?' and... nothing. They sympathize with the dogs and think they're just putting them in a safe place and that's it. Now it's our burden to take care of them along with all of the others."

I took the opportunity to ask Mona the question I had wanted an answer to for 7 years. "Now... were you worried I was going to do that when I first contacted you?"

She paused. "No. Because the video itself. Whether you were going to take her or not, we wouldn't have left her on the streets." She pointed down at the two Mohamed had just let out. "There was nothing wrong with them. They were this shape, just on the streets."

That's the sad reality of the situation. In the U.S., we call in a stray dog sighting and expect it to get picked up no matter what, not just the injured ones. In Egypt, there are so many that if they're in fine health the rescues simply can't afford to take them.

Two dogs had been trailing us the length of the hall, neither could use their back legs. "She came paralyzed. She was probably hit by a car and left on the streets for a long time. All her lower part was injured, now it's…" she made a motion with her hand, "a bit better. Her name is Elaina." There was a black one with the same problem next to her. "Muffin."

As it turns out, Mona and Heidi both know the name of just about every single dog. They know their story, when they came in, and how long they've been there. The commitment and dedication is impressive.

We exited a gate at the end of the hall back into the main lobby. There were three more runs with cage doors to the left. "This is where Sphinx stayed," Mona said, pointing to the first door.

I stood there looking in at the current occupants. Four dogs, one of which was thrilled to see us. Licking our hands through the bars, craving human contact.

Seeing that run in person brought the whole thing together for me. I had seen pictures of Sphyncus looking out of those exact bars almost 7 years ago. For whatever reason, I had felt like I always needed to see it. I needed to know exactly where she had been those two months between when I left her in front of the hotel and picked her up at the airport. Throughout the day, I felt myself being continuously pulled back to that cage door as if by some gravitational force.

Before too long, the rest of my "ESMA family" arrived. Kris Shultz with Mohamed El-bebawy, Anne-Marie, Lia, and Bahra. Bahra told a story about how on her way out to the shelter she saw some kids on a scooter dragging a puppy, but she was able to stop them and get the dog. It horrified me that on any given day, at any given time, something like that could happen and it was totally normal. It took Bahra a little while to shake it off and attempt to enjoy the festivities. No matter how many times she had seen something like that, it was still damaging every single time.

Over the course of the afternoon, I met a few more important ESMA people for the first time. A Scottish expat named Christina Webb, who is a 'Jack of all trades' for ESMA. A tank of a man named Mohamed Tawfik. A woman named Anna Anderswie from Germany that's worked with ESMA for years and helps with adoptions in Europe. Two photographers named Sherif El Kadi and Maged El Din. A man I only know as John that works at the Cairo airport and helps with the process of flying the animals. I was told he would be helping me on Monday when I flew home.

One of the sweetest people I've ever met in my life is a tiny older woman named Seham Saneya Abd El Salam. She's an actress and we'd been friends online for a few years. She ventured all the way out to the ESMA shelter specifically to meet me. I felt like a celebrity. She came right up and gave me a big hug.

Lunch was provided in the afternoon and it was my first time ever eating the Egyptian dish koshary. Koshary is a traditional Egyptian dish made from lentils, rice, and macaroni mixed together, and topped with tomato sauce, oil, onions, chickpeas, hot sauce, and spices. It's amazing. Tables were set up in the building I had tirelessly cleaned the day before and the food was being served out of one of the smaller rooms. It all suddenly made sense why we needed to get that building so spotless.

Two singers, a female I would later get to know as Dema Nagi, and a male whose name I never learned, began singing karaoke. They traded off every couple of songs and went well into the evening. People were dancing with each other, dancing with dogs, singing along, it was one big party. If I wasn't so self-conscious about it, I would have loved to have danced or sang something if there were any songs I knew.

Late in the afternoon, Mona took the microphone to give a speech. She periodically switched back and forth between Arabic and English telling the story of ESMA and thanking everyone that had ever been involved, whether they were present or not. Going down an endless mental list, everybody got their shout out with an explanation of the role they've played over the years. I stood at the back of the crowd taking video of it like I was in a hall of heroes, documenting their tales and triumphs. These people were legends. The highest quality of humans to exist.

About ten minutes into the speech, Mona started talking about all the people that have supported from overseas and mentioned America. "And today we have people representing the U.S. people. Josh Hines, one of the people supporting ESMA and also adopter of one of the very, very famous stories of dogs that we rescued, Sphinx, the very famous Sphinx girl." As she continued to tell Sphyncus' story, everyone in the crowd stared and applauded me. I don't know if I've ever been so uncomfortable or felt so unworthy of praise in my life.

What I had done was one thing for one dog 7 years ago, I didn't belong in the same conversation as anyone there that day. They are the true champions of animal rescue. I was a bystander that got involved purely by chance. I was incredibly honored. Being appreciated and welcomed by that crowd of people, none of whom I had met more than a few days or hours before, was recognition that I don't feel I had earned. I'll be eternally grateful to Mona and everyone in attendance that day.

At the end of the speech, Mona said something that got right in my heart. "One last thank you is to every ESMA dog, cat, donkey, horse, any animal that came into ESMA that give us the privilege to be more human. More caring. More loving. They have taught us what love is, unconditional love. Every ESMA animal has taught us unconditional love. We love you all for giving us the chance to help you. We love you all for giving us the chance to be what we are now. And we love you more for making the name of ESMA. So, to all our dogs living with us, adopted in their homes, or up there in heaven, thank you very, very, very much every one. I know you understand me. I know you can really understand and hear what I say."

She then switched to Arabic to finish it out. Finally, she kissed a locket on her neck that had a picture of Antar, her dog soulmate that had passed a few years earlier, and waved to the crowd. With tears in her eyes she went to Lia for a hug as everyone applauded. I'll never forget it for as long as I live.

When it came time to leave, Dareen offered to drive Kris, Mohamed El-bebawy, and me since most

Ubers wouldn't come all the way out to the shelter. Traffic was getting especially thick in the city so Dareen wasn't able to take us each back to our hotels. She dropped us all off on a corner where an Uber would be able to get us and then went on her way. She'd been an essential part of my time in Cairo and that was the last I ever saw of her. Leaving the dog shelter was the last I would see of the most of the people I'd come to know and rely on so heavily.

By the time I got back to the Lofts I was exhausted. Kris called me later in the night and tried to coax me back out with her and Mohamed, but with how thick the traffic was and how long of a day it had been I politely declined. I almost settled on eating snacks in the room and going to bed, but around midnight I found my adventurous spirit had returned and decided to go out looking for food. Rather than calling another Uber, I chose to walk until I found something.

Before leaving, my family and friends all told me repeatedly "be safe, don't go out alone, don't go out at night, don't do anything stupid" and I was about to do every one of those things all at the same time. Maybe the first night or two of being there I wouldn't have been ballsy enough to go for a midnight stroll alone in that part of Cairo, but after five days of never feeling remotely unsafe or threatened I thought I could handle myself.

The biggest difference I saw between night and day in Cairo was all the baladi dogs came out at night. I hadn't seen many roaming around until that walk. They were everywhere, rooting through trash, barking, and living their nocturnal desert lives. They gave me no reason to fear them even when walking past large groups. Once again, all the concerns the girl in 2010 had told me about were completely unfounded when going by my own personal experiences.

After about five minutes of walking I came upon a small diner with the lights on and a man hanging around outside. A few minutes later there was a feast spread out before me. A plate with a large roll of bread and several pita pockets, another with fries and falafel balls, a bowl of ful, a bowl of hummus, a small salad, another bowl of some type of sauce, a bottle of water, and a Pepsi. I had no idea where I was going to fit all of that in my body, but it wouldn't stop me from trying. I haven't been a soda drinker in probably 15 years but by God I chugged that Pepsi down. Everything was delicious. That meal is when I knew how much I was really going to miss everything about Egyptian food when I went back home. The entire thing was less than a hundred pounds, around five U.S. dollars.

I walked back to the room and settled in. It had been a hell of a day. Probably one of the best of my life. Per my nightly ritual, I opened the window in case my little orange friend decided to drop by.

Chapter 26

Waking up Saturday, I decided that my last 2 days in Egypt weren't going to be spent working. Despite that being the primary reason I went to Cairo, I still had friends to meet up with and I wanted to see a little bit more of the city, too.

Before heading out, I spent some time on the roof of Pyramids Loft and ran into Mohamed, the right-hand man of the place. I asked him about the orange cat that had become my roommate and he informed me he was the hotel cat. His name was Mishmish and he takes to going in open windows to sleep with guests, particularly solo travelers. I had grown attached to Mishmish and was concerned that I wouldn't be able to leave him behind if he was just a stray.

After playing phone tag all week long, I headed out to finally meet up with one of my best Egyptian friends, a young woman named Louby Farag. We met up for coffee then went to her apartment to walk her dogs, Lucy and Vodka.

While walking the area around her building, she made sure to keep reminding me to not let Vodka sniff any one spot too long--there might be a morsel of food around and the poisoning of dogs is a big problem in the area. Snapping back to reality, I remembered where I was and what was sadly considered normal. Government officials deny involvement in it, but there are organized poisonings of neighborhoods periodically. The target is obviously the strays, but any animal can fall prey to it if they find the remains on the ground. Vodka is a big, strong German Shepherd that I had just met. I didn't want to be too forceful with her and thankfully she was very obedient. Louby had clearly disciplined her to not linger too long and get any ideas but she was still a dog. I had to watch her carefully.

As we got back to Louby's apartment, a woman in a black jilbab (the long and loose outer garment worn by some Muslim women that still leaves the face exposed) walked past, triggering Lucy to start barking. The woman looked terrified. She sped up and ranted at us in Arabic, looking madder and madder with each word that came out. I'd never seen such an overreaction before, especially to a tiny little Yorkie yipping.

On my sixth day in Cairo I finally saw the type of attitude towards animals I had been expecting all along. After all the animal lovers I'd been around and all of the animals themselves, all I could think was "what an idiot." Her life would be all the more empty for viewing the world that way and not experiencing the love of dogs. It was like a portal opened, revealing the Cairo of 2010.

My Uber arrived and finally the guy's name wasn't Mohamed, but he didn't speak a word of English either. You win some, you lose some. Since we couldn't speak to each other at all, we listened to the radio and he took one phone call after another. Traffic was thick and eventually came to a standstill. It took about two hours to get from Louby's place to Khan el-Khalili where I was meeting Kris Shultz and Mohamed El-Bebawy. The two hour long Uber ride cost less than 5 US dollars.

Khan el-Khalili is a giant bazaar that's centuries old, full of vendors selling everything known to man.

Street after street making a labyrinth of merchants and shops peddling clothing, antiques, souvenirs, jewelry, food, and trinkets. You name it and it can probably be found in the Khan. Kris told me to meet her at El-Fishawi, located somewhere near the center.

Smoky El-Fishawi is the oldest café in Cairo and it feels like something out of an old movie. Indiana Jones could be hanging out in there somewhere. I've been to a lot of ancient sites all over the world, but you can literally feel the history around you in that café. It was worth the trouble to get to it.

Kris, Mohamed, and I explored the Khan for a while. It's an amazing place I couldn't believe I had missed on my first visit to Egypt. We had apparently been close by at the Egyptian Museum, but Sphyncus breaking my heart had prevented us from wanting to explore any further. I can only imagine how we would have behaved in there with the negative attitude we were lugging around.

Kris told me she couldn't get Mohamed up and active until around 2 p.m. His response was "In Egypt, if the sun is up it's still morning. It's so hot during the day." He said Egyptians are somewhat unorganized as a people and time doesn't mean the same thing to them as most other places. They don't spend all their time looking at their watches. I somewhat envied that casual attitude toward life.

Eventually we came to Old Cairo, which has some of the most beautiful architecture I've ever seen. You can really appreciate the intricacies and curvature of Arabic architecture when it's surrounding you on all sides. I was entranced by it. Before heading out, I bought Sphyncus an Eye of Horus charm to go on her collar to bring a little of the motherland back to my girl.

The three of us met up with Heidi Alsabban at a restaurant for koshary. We picked up a friend of hers and proceeded to close out various coffee shops again like we had a few nights before. Most of the cafes and bars we'd been to all had a large selection of board games, so Heidi gave me my first taste of Egyptian backgammon.

I love backgammon and I'm going to toot my own horn to tell you that I'm pretty good at it. Louby and I had planned to play long before I ever actually made the trip over, but we got sidetracked and ran out of time. I figured all the trash I had talked to Louby about playing would transfer right over to Heidi, but she outright destroyed me the first game we played. I was stunned.

Being a Hines means you can't stand losing, so Heidi gave me a chance to earn some of my pride back. I barely beat her the next two games but by official backgammon scoring we were tied. We decided to play the tiebreaker my next trip over. After getting lost again on the ride back to the Loft, Heidi dropped me off a little after 5 a.m.

Sunday was my last day, but I slept in until noon anyway. Aside from how late I'd stayed out, little Mishmish had crawled in bed with me one last time. I was going to miss the little guy. There was nothing planned aside from sorting out the flight parent situation with Mona and maybe trying to meet up with another person that I hadn't gotten to see yet.

For the longest time, I didn't know much about Phaedra Al-Masri other than my internet interactions with her. I didn't even know her real name as she doesn't use it online. She looked glamorous in a lot of her pictures and she posted things about being 'on set' so I put it together that she's an actress. An actual actress had friended me because of Sphyncus. She would comment on my dog pictures and frequently encouraged me when going through struggles with E-Style. She got a kick out of me thinking her real name was actually Sheeba so the first time she called me in Cairo I was greeted with "Hey Josh, it's Sheeba" followed by laughter. We decided to meet up with Louby for dinner that evening.

Shortly after, Mona called me and said her and Mohamed Tawfik were taking me and Kris to dinner on the Nile at 8 p.m. so my open day suddenly turned into a busy, jam packed last night in Egypt where I had to somehow eat two dinners.

At the first restaurant, the staff clearly recognized Phaedra. Nobody approached but I caught the waiters looking. That dinner made me realize how bizarre my life had become over the past week. I was in a country I swore I'd never go back to eating dinner with a famous Arabic actress. I had met at least 20 Mohameds. I had barely paid for anything all week. A random hotel cat slept in my bed with me every night. And in a couple of hours, I'd be eating again on the Nile with the founder of ESMA, who also is a presenter on Egyptian TV. And in the morning, I'd be flying seven dogs to the U.S. All because I had grown too attached to an injured street dog 7 years ago. Real life was unrecognizable, and my years of depression felt like ancient history.

I lost track of time and the next thing I knew it was close to 8 o'clock. The Nile was at least 45 minutes away from our present location. I didn't want to disappoint Mona but at the same time it would only be appropriate if the last place I had to go I showed up late to. Like 'hey guys, I finally learned how it works over here!'

A funny thing happened while on the way to Nile City. My driver actually spoke English. The last one I would have and I could finally talk to him. As we got closer to downtown the traffic got insane as usual and he started laughing. He asked if I had ever seen traffic like this anywhere in the world. I told him only once before; the first time I came to Cairo. We both got a good laugh out of it. I tipped him all of my remaining Egyptian Pounds.

A little before 9, I walked into Nile City. The restaurant is literally a boat sitting right on the Nile. Amazing when you think about it. Mona, Mohamed Tawfik, Kris, and Mohamed El-babawy were already there. My plan to show up late and still be early failed. I felt like an ass.

Shortly after, Heidi Alsabban showed up. It was appropriate to spend my last night with that group. Through the two late nights we'd spent together, plus the ESMA anniversary party, I viewed Heidi, Kris, and Mohamed as my Cairo family. Our little fantastic four.

Dinner with Mona Khalil was a great opportunity to get to know her better as a human being and not just as the face of ESMA. She's a very strong woman. Still somewhat conservative, but for a Muslim woman she is very independent and confident. I could see where some men could possibly be intimidated by her, but I found her very friendly and pleasant to be around.

I know I've said something similar to this numerous times already, but having dinner with Mona was surreal. She's a literal hero to me. Over the years and through all the delays that came up, every time I thought about visiting there was a piece of me that was curious if I'd ever actually do it. If the internet friendships I had would ever exist in the real physical world. By the end of my time in Cairo, one of the biggest heroes I've ever had was my close personal friend.

Mona and Tawfik paid for everything and made sure there was plenty of food for me to eat, the lone vegetarian of the group. I was their guest, so everything was their treat. Incredible hospitality. Toward the end of dinner, they pulled out a fat wad of cash and started counting it. They passed it down to me and asked me to count it again.

$1,400. That was to pay for the dogs I was flying with. Only $300 more than Sphyncus cost alone. It showed the true value of acting as a flight parent. $200 per dog if you merely claim responsibility for them rather than $1,100 to fly a single dog as cargo. All of ESMA's pleas for flight parents made more sense than ever.

Mona told me Mido would be picking me up at my hotel around 5 a.m with the dogs. 6 of them I wouldn't see again until landing in Chicago, the other would be in a small, soft crate with me in the cabin. My little flight buddy was named Miro, the dog I had referred to as 'fat puppy Sphyncus' from my first day at the cat shelter. It felt like fate.

The other dogs that would be coming with me were three sisters known as The Spice Girls (Cinnamon, Paprika, and Curry), a friendly but nervous tripod I'd met at the anniversary named Latifa, a black dog named Merlot, and the puppy that Dareen was carrying around at the anniversary party named Mimi.

Around 10:30 P.M. we made for the door. My pick up was less than 7 hours away and I still wasn't fully packed. Heidi jumped in "No! You have to take a felucca ride! There is some food you still need to try, traditional Egyptian food!"

I resisted and looked around for somebody to back me up. It was going to be a long flight early in the morning and I had to tote around a little fat puppy Sphyncus for the entirety of it, surely everyone agreed that I needed to get some sleep. Nope. Even Mona smiled and encouraged me to go all out for my last night in Egypt. "You can sleep on the plane," she said. So, it was decided. Mona and Tawfik went on their way and my little Cairo family walked to Heidi's car.

I have to admit that I really enjoyed going out and I'm glad I didn't put up a fight about it. The felucca ride was a peaceful experience and doing it at night, on my last night in the country, made it even more beautiful. We had it all to ourselves, too. Kris, Mohamed, Heidi, me, and the driver. A family outing.

Cairo around the Nile is lit up like any other big city along a body of water - lights, high rises, and neon signs. Mohamed sat at the front of the boat and dangled his legs off so I joined him, sitting by the side rail. Kris and Heidi came up about halfway through the ride. It was one of those times where if it weren't for a handful of particular things and people back home, I could have been content to just stay there with my new family.

Once we docked, Heidi took us to try some Egyptian sweets before we ended up at a packed hookah bar around 2 a.m. For a late Sunday night, Cairo was alive. I still couldn't get over how normal it was in comparison to American cities' nightlife. A far cry from what I had expected and experienced before. I loved the new Cairo I'd been introduced to. We weren't able to stay long before I played the role of party pooper and reminded everyone I had a plane to catch in a few hours. It was difficult telling Kris and Mohamed goodbye. I knew I'd be back and would see them again, but I didn't know when. Mohamed had become my new brother. I didn't know him a week earlier, but he'd been incredibly good to me and we had a lot in common. We shared a lot of the same views despite the two different worlds we live in.

We all joke about having a 'second mom' growing up, like your best friend's mom or a band mom, and Kris had come to feel like my second mom. She's probably only 10 to 15 years older than me, but for somebody that doesn't have kids Kris is a solid parental figure. My real mom would be thankful I had her.

Heidi drove me back to the Lofts for the third time that week and got lost on the way for the third time. It was getting hilarious. The buildings and streets all blended together but I swear we somehow took the same unintentional path every time. Around 4 A.M. we pulled up to the Lofts. I had one hour to get my shit together before Mido would be arriving. I gave her a hug and she looked sad, almost like she wanted to cry but wouldn't dare. My Egyptian sister with the beautiful voice.

I went to my room hoping to see Mishmish asleep on the bed, but he was nowhere to be found. I guess he doesn't care for sleeping alone so had made his way somewhere else. Next time, Mishmish. Next time.

I showered and packed up the rest of my stuff then realized I had a decent amount of food left. Throughout the week I had seen baladi dogs rooting through a big trash pile close to the Pyramids Light Show entrance, so I opened up my remaining food and sat it down on the sidewalk. I had just enough time to get back on the roof of the Loft and take in one final Egyptian sunrise over the Pyramids. Magnificent.

Mido showed up 30 minutes late because it couldn't possibly end any other way. At the airport he and one of the guys from the painting crew put the crates together on the sidewalk and loaded the dogs up two to a crate. He handed me a stack of puppy pads for my little fat puppy Sphyncus, Miro, and we all said goodbye.

The man known as John that I had met at ESMA's anniversary party was waiting for me by the airport entrance. He asked for the money, my passport, and the paperwork for the dogs, then took care of everything else. I just stood with Miro not doing anything.

John had one final parting gift for me – I got to choose, right there on the spot, where I wanted to sit on every plane on my way home. I don't know much about John other than he works at the Cairo airport and helps ESMA out but whatever pull he has at the airport was a godsend to my tired eyes. Having a window seat made sleeping easier and it also helped with keeping Miro tucked away without people possibly kicking his crate as they moved around in the cabin. Mona was one hundred percent accurate in how it would go down. They took care of everything. I'd been so nervous and worried about what the process would be like, but it was just so simple and stress free.

John came up to me before I went through security. "Here is my number, please call me right before you get on so we can confirm the dogs are on the plane. When you get to Germany please ask them to confirm the dogs are on the plane again before taking off to America. Call me if there are any problems at all. Thank you for what you're doing." He flashed one of the most genuine smiles I'd ever seen. I was confused by him thanking me. I wasn't doing anything but going home.

Everyone put forth such effort to make sure I was comfortable and on the right track without any worries. The Egyptian people from 2017 were so drastically different from those I'd met in 2010. It might as well have been two entirely different places. The ultimate redemption story. I was no longer the dumb tourist caring too much for a filthy baladi dog. I was among friends that saw the value and love in all animals. Likeminded people that didn't laugh when I pet a dog. I didn't hear "Welcome to Egypt" once all week.

For the second time in my life when I got on the plane to go home from Cairo, I truly felt sad to be leaving.

## Chapter 27

When I had boarded the flight from Chicago to Vienna a week earlier, I talked about all of the empty seats in the back of the plane that turned out to be too good to be true. As luck would have it, on my flight from Cairo to Frankfurt, when I needed it the most after pulling an all-nighter, my entire row was empty. It was only a three-and-a-half-hour flight, but I stretched across all three seats and fell into a coma. Fat puppy Sphyncus snoozed in his crate on the floor without making a sound.

Upon landing in Frankfurt, I could tell my little puppy friend had gone through his first pee pad. Kris had given me good advice on how to handle the layover —find a bathroom with stall doors that went all the way to the floor and just hang out in one a little while so the dog could stretch his legs a bit. It also gave me a chance to get him cleaned up and change out his old pad. We were down to two.

Miro started to get a little whiny on me in the stall. He was very young and needed a lot of sleep. He barely walked around before climbing on top of my backpack and sprawling out. I was getting hungry and my little dude wasn't interested in his free time, so I went back to the area around my gate to find food. It wasn't long after sitting down with some pretzels that fat puppy Sphyncus started making grunt sounds and shifting around a lot. We hadn't been out of the bathroom stall for five minutes and he'd pooped in his crate. Awesome.

I got him cleaned up a second time and left him out longer. He still only wanted to lay on my backpack. Down to our last pee pad, we went back out to the gate. Wouldn't you know it, before they called us up to board the little pee pants did his thing in there again. The layover was only a couple hours and he hadn't drank any water. I guess it was just being nervous and being a puppy. Either way, I was out of pee pads. I took two plain white shirts out of my bag, the ones I had worn while painting and cleaning the shelters, folded them up, and laid them down inside. I was concerned about the long flight to Chicago and if the person next to me would make a fuss about it.

While standing in line to board, I met a nice older couple that took an interest in Miro and what I had been doing in Egypt. They offered their help but I had to decline, there was literally nothing they could do, at least not yet.

For the most part, Miro was calm and quiet throughout the flight. Having that window seat meant I nodded off repeatedly. Miro clearly peed in the crate again and there was a faint smell hanging around but nobody complained. I felt bad for him, but there was nothing I could do. I had no other old clothes to give him and, even if I did, it would be difficult to get them out of my backpack in the overhead bin. My bag was packed to the point of explosion so I couldn't mess with stuffing everything back in there in the aisle.

At baggage claim in Chicago, I found the three big crates waiting for me by the back wall. I stacked two on one push cart and needed a second cart for the third. All the while I had a bulging bag weighing at least twenty pounds on my back with little Miro's soft crate hanging over my shoulder. No workers offered a hand or gave me a second look. Attempting to push two of those carts at the same time with their uneven weight distribution was not easy. Latifa the tripod was panicking and knocked her crate over several times causing a ruckus that got a lot of staring. Merlot was in another crate and had become aggressive toward me if I got too close to the door. The stress must have taken away her sweet nature.

Fortunately, the friendly older woman from Vienna saw me struggling and came over to help me push them up to the last security check before having to go back to her husband. The guys at the final checkpoint were friendly, asking about the dogs and what it was like for them in Egypt. Knowing that Kris primarily flew out of O'Hare and always brought animals back, I was confident at least one of those men had seen ESMA paperwork before. They let me pass quickly and two of them even helped push the carts outside.

My contact from Cascades Humane Society, Jeff Henkel, pulled up in his van and we loaded the crates into the back. He had driven down three and a half hours from Jackson, Michigan to pick up the dogs and would be driving straight back up. It takes a lot of love and dedication to make a seven hour round trip that late at night.

I put little fat puppy Sphyncus in the passenger seat. I'd grown quite fond of him, but I knew I couldn't take him home. I wasn't ready for another dog just yet.

Seven ESMA dogs were being given a chance to get adopted and have families. To live normal dog lives.

Spoiled, sleeping on beds in the air conditioning, running in the grass, and getting all the one-on-one attention they deserve. Seven dogs rescued from the unforgiving streets. Seven dogs whose departure meant ESMA had room for seven more. If nothing else, I felt good about playing a role in that. The painting and the cleaning could have all been done without me. Getting these dogs to America was something I was needed for. Something I could look back on and know I had done a good thing. Counting Sphyncus, there were eight Egyptian dogs in America because of me. I had always imagined Sphyncus alone would be my legacy, but maybe there was more.

I went back inside and boarded the plane to Nashville. As the final flight of my journey took off, it gave me an opportunity to reflect on everything I had been through. Knowing I was returning home to my daily grind, the last week already felt like an alternate universe.

Which Egypt had I traveled to? Was the Egypt of 2010 the real Egypt or was it the one of 2017? Did people "drive over him without drive over him" or did they dance with dogs at anniversary parties? Was it "now is time for giving me tips if you like" or was I a guest that wasn't allowed to pay for anything? "Are you happy? Make me happy" or "as you like?" Was the treatment of stray animals "Welcome to Egypt" or was it knowing the name and backstory of over 500 individual dogs? Were animals kicked in the streets or did they climb in your hotel window? Had I sworn to never return or was I already planning my next trip back? Some of these questions I can answer myself, but questions regarding what is the real Egypt can only be answered by the Egyptian people themselves and what kind of future they want to have.

The one connecting link between the two different Egypts I had experienced was Sphyncus. My baladi. There is no story without her. I would have no Egyptian friends without her. No heroes to meet. No actresses to go to dinner with. No Cairo family to close out bars with. For all I knew Egyptian weasels would have bones.

There would be no redemption without Sphyncus. No return. I wouldn't have ever gone back to the place that so thoroughly shredded my heart into pieces only to ultimately fall in love with that same place. I wouldn't have fallen in love with a nation of people that I once thought of as the scum of the Earth. When I was at my lowest, darkest point, Egypt pulled me up from the depths. When I needed to change who I was in order to be happy again, Egypt was there to remind me not to give up. The person that went to Egypt is not the same person that came back. I returned home inspired and humbled.

Twice in my life when I needed a light at the end of the tunnel, ESMA shone brightest. In a land that gives them absolutely nothing but adversity every step of the way, ESMA is fighting every single day for the betterment of animals. Taking in the sick, the injured, the dying, the starving, the abandoned, the unwanted. Funded by donations and run mostly by volunteers. The type of people we should all aspire to be. Hard workers that won't accept that things can't be better. People with endless love to give. People not afraid to speak up.

When I first visited Cairo, I was under the impression that what I was seeing was normal, and in a sense it is, but that doesn't mean it's accepted by everyone as the way things should be. The loudest voices are sometimes the nastiest. All the good things being done can easily be overshadowed by the bad. I thought Egypt was nothing but nasty and bad, but I was wrong. Egypt is amazing and its people are beautiful. The horrible few cannot be allowed to have a louder voice than the beautiful many.

Egypt must enact laws to protect its stray animal population from torment and cruelty. There's no reason ordinary people should be able to commit atrocities right out in the open. Things that would be considered serious crimes and make national news in other parts of the world are just every day occurrences in Egypt. It can't remain that way. Egypt must educate its young people on the value of animals and having a positive relationship with them. They must learn that a stray doesn't always signal trouble or danger.

It's not out of the realm of possibility for Egypt to implement a spay/neuter and release system, rather than the barbarism of poisoning and shooting. Government funding would help animal shelters function better, thus getting more animals off the streets. Egyptian people need to understand that having a purebred dog or cat is not a status symbol; it's not recognized as luxurious to any rational thinking person. A dog is a dog and a cat is a cat. Compassion is worth more than the money to buy a purebred.

Americans, and people all over the world for that matter, have our share of issues when it comes to respecting animals. Factory farming is an unnecessary cruelty and puppy mills are an abomination. My home state of Kentucky is an embarrassment to the nation with our slap on the wrist laws towards animal cruelty. We are all better than this. As human beings we have the ability to reason like no other creature on this Earth. We can find better ways to share this planet with those that can't speak up for themselves. Not everyone has to adopt a vegetarian or vegan diet but there is no need for the horrible conditions millions of animals spend their entire lives in just because we are lazy and place a premium on convenience. We're better than that.

There are millions of animals at shelters and on the streets at any given time all over the world. Anyone could do the same things I've done. I'm nobody special and I've not done anything extraordinary. Maybe most people wouldn't be up for the entire ordeal of bringing a dog home from overseas, but there are animals in every city that have suffered that anyone could adopt at any moment.

It took me traveling abroad to find the dog I was supposed to be with, whereas it might take somebody else just a quick drive down to their local humane society. My soulmate might have been a Chinese Crested show dog, but I was also meant to have a baladi from Cairo. I'm a better man for every dog I've ever known.

If there's anyone out there that is curious about baladi dogs and cats and is inspired to give one a chance, please by all means at least look into it. If nothing else, please consider donating time or money to any animal shelter, whether it be ESMA or your local humane society. There is never enough money and always too many animals to care for. I can tell you from personal experience that a shelter dog will love you like no other. You literally saved their life and they know it and they will thank you for as long as they live. You can't buy that kind of unconditional love at a store. They all have their own unique story just waiting to share with someone.

Sphyncus is by no means a perfect dog. She's extremely stubborn when she wants to be, she doesn't warm up to new people or animals at all, she's very territorial about her home and our neighborhood, and her behavior is the very definition of unpredictable. She barks at everything, she barks at nothing, she chases everything, she tries to herd me and the other animals where she wants us to go, she follows me everywhere, and she stands behind me so I can't move.

She's wild as hell, always on high alert, she scratches things, chews things up, she ran off with a cell phone, and she has to crawl through Batcaves and under chairs and squeeze between the table and the wall rather than using the entire open room. She's very deliberate in keeping habits. She freaks out over everything. She's terrified of fireworks and high pitch beeping and all frequencies in between. She slides across slick floors and goes around corners backwards. She's just insanely weird. A very strange and frustrating dog. I love her so much.

She's incredibly unique. She's really funny and she knows it. Every day is a comedy show. She's playful and is always up for exploring outside, no matter the weather. She's the sweetest dog ever, even though she's not a cuddler most of the time. She's extremely smart. She was somehow housebroken immediately and learns commands quickly. She's clumsy and it's hilarious. There's nothing in the world like coming home to a wiggle worm. She's overly protective but you can't complain about that. She's the most loyal creature I've ever encountered. Her nose is always wet and she loves to touch you with it. She won't let me out of her sight. She has to know what I'm doing and be involved in it. There's never a dull moment. I just love her so much.

She's changed me as a person entirely. I spend so much time outdoors now, no matter what season it is. I've been to places in my hometown that I never knew even knew existed because of her. Just going out and finding places to go and things to do. Every single day I look forward to coming home and seeing what we can get into. Sphyncus is fearful, yet absolutely fearless. She is my proudest accomplishment. Watching her go from a timid, scrawny, pitiful little thing to the confident, healthy, energized, playful, hilarious, happy, smiling dog that she became is the greatest feeling of success I have ever known.

The agony, the uncertainty, the pain, the tears... I wouldn't change a thing. The entire process destroyed my faith in humanity only to restore it to new heights. The cruelty of strangers and the generosity of strangers. I don't believe in God and I don't believe in fate, but I do believe that somehow in the randomness of existence, Sphyncus and I were supposed to find each other. It was our destiny.

I know I get long winded, this book is proof of it, but Sphyncus listens to everything I have to say with that one ear up. I tell her story often, every time we meet a stranger, and she stands proudly beside me knowing she's the star of the show. She's always full of facial expressions and at times she almost looks embarrassed when I gloat on her too much. Other times, she's got too many squirrels to chase and will continuously pull on her leash so I can't stand around having a long conversation with somebody on the street corner.

And sometimes, I'm simply just not up to getting into the whole thing and answering a bunch of questions —like I'm exaggerating or making it up. On those rare days, whenever I don't feel like going through the entire story, I just tell people that I'm like Zeus and Sphyncus is like Athena—she simply sprang forth from my forehead fully grown and in her battle armor. My baladi.

*Baladi*

## ABOUT THE AUTHOR

Josh Hines is an animal rights advocate, rescuer, fund raiser, volunteer, and web administrator for the Egyptian Society for Mercy to Animals. Since 2017 he is personally responsible for flying 14 Egyptian baladi dogs to the United States to rescues and new homes. He has worked in TV news since 2007, traveled to over 20 countries across five continents, and released somewhere around 50 albums with various bands. Josh returns to Egypt every year to volunteer for the ESMA shelter and act as a flight parent to dogs. He currently lives in his hometown of Bowling Green, KY with his wife and their ever-growing family of rescued and stray animals.